# SILENT PILGRIMAGE TO GOD

*The Spirituality of Charles de Foucauld*

# SILENT PILGRIMAGE
# TO GOD

*The Spirituality of Charles de Foucauld*

## BY A LITTLE BROTHER OF JESUS

translated by
JEREMY MOISER

Preface by
RENÉ VOILLAUME

ORBIS BOOKS
Maryknoll, New York 10545

Originally published as
*Ce Que Croyait Charles de Foucauld*
by Maison Mame, Paris

Copyright © 1974 Darton, Longman and Todd, London

Library of Congress Catalog Card Number: 74-32516
Cloth Edition, 1975
Cloth ISBN 0-88344-459-3

Paperbound Edition, 1977
Paperbound ISBN 0-88344-461-5

Manufactured in the United States of America


Third Printing, January 1981

# CONTENTS

Preface                                                    7
Note                                                       9
Introduction                                              11


*Part One* – THE FAITH OF BROTHER CHARLES

The Gift of Faith                                         15
Living and Active Faith                                   19


*Part Two* – THE GREAT INSIGHTS OF HIS FAITH

Jesus of Nazareth                                         28
Jesus Christ in the Eucharist                             31
The Happiness of God                                      35
Shouting the Gospel from the housetop of one's
   life                                                   38
The Gospel phrase which transformed my life               42
He was called Jesus, which means Saviour                  45
The Source of Joy                                         49
Everything that unites us to the Church unites
   us to Jesus                                            51
Our Lady and the Saints                                   54
Sainte-Baume in the Hoggar                                57

My Father who is also your Father 61
Why Death? 63
Conclusion 66


*Part Three* – EXTRACTS FROM THE WRITINGS OF
BROTHER CHARLES OF JESUS

Meditation on self-abasement 71
Jesus in the Holy Eucharist 73
The happiness of the Beloved 75
To follow in poverty a God of poverty 76
Like Jesus at Nazareth 77
Whatever you do to one of the least of these
  brothers of mine . . . 79
On slavery 80
The Good Shepherd 81
Union with the Church 82
The Church on the evening of SS Peter and
  Paul's martyrdom 82
Meditation on the Visitation 83
Mary Magdalene 84
Alone with Jesus 85
To make up all that has still to be undergone
  by Christ 86
Your thought of death 87


*Part Four*

Short Biography of Brother Charles of Jesus 91
Bibliography 94
Notes 96

# PREFACE

It has become a commonplace to say that faith today is more difficult than it has ever been. Some even conclude that it can no longer mean to us what it once meant to those Christians who, throughout the Church's history, have been the incontestable witnesses to the vigour of the faith – the 'divine force', as St Paul calls the Gospel – and to the transformation a living faith can bring to human existence.

Such a transfiguration of man is possible only if faith seizes the very heart of his being and renews his powers of knowing, loving and acting. Faith would hardly be worth the having if it did not, by its very nature, bestow a growth of being, an added dimension to life, because it is a real possession of the True and Living God and the gifts he has created. If faith were merely a 'language to be interpreted', as it is sometimes said today, it would be powerless to transfigure men's lives.

The reality of the world which faith alone affirms is not subject to rational demonstration or scientific experimentation. But in our day even its human approach encounters a new difficulty which sometimes amounts to an almost insuperable obstacle. It is the result of a mentality that refuses to believe in purely spiritual beings and in realities of which our senses have no immediate grasp.

There remains, however, the incontestable strength, grandeur and beauty of the lives of witnesses who have

7

lived fully 'as if they saw the invisible'. Charles de Foucauld is one of the greatest of these witnesses who are close to us in time. His life can be explained at all only on the supposition that it was inspired totally by faith; otherwise it is quite meaningless. Those who have been granted the grace to know him and make him their spiritual guide know by experience the fulness they receive when they steep their lives in the warmth and light of Brother Charles of Jesus' great faith.

At a time when 'sharing' is again one of the key values of the Christian community, how could we not wish to share, with those who want to, these spiritual gifts which God has seen fit to lavish on us?

This unpretentious book, written by a Little Brother of Jesus who has been a disciple of Charles de Foucauld for more than thirty years, is designed simply to let Brother Charles witness to his faith with the strength, simplicity and love that characterise it. Commentary would merely weaken this witness. We know by experience that Brother Charles of Jesus cannot fail to encourage Christians who wish to follow their 'Beloved Brother and Lord' more closely in charity, the spirit of evangelical poverty and prayer.

RENÉ VOILLAUME

*Algiers, 25 March 1971*

# NOTE

In quotations from the writings of Charles de Foucauld, the capitals, emphases and ellipses of the original have been respected. Cuts in the text are indicated by three points in parenthesis.

# INTRODUCTION

The life of Charles de Foucauld is well known, and various selections of his spiritual writings and correspondence have been published. The following study is an attempt to clarify the motivation behind his chosen life as a hermit in the African desert.

His was a rough road, and he embarked on it when he decided to devote all his energies to God: was he to do less for God than he had done for his country and for science? To carry out his scientific researches he had risked life and limb in two years of heroic courage. For God he would attempt the impossible!

A remark of Fr Huvelin's is illuminating: 'The beauty of the goal to which he felt himself called hid all the rest from him, especially the unachievable.'[1]

He himself wrote on 14 August 1901: 'If our religion is the truth, if the Gospel is the word of God, we must believe and put it into practice, even if we are absolutely the only ones to do so.'[2]

And he left for the desert, alone.

\* \* \*

In the first part of this study we shall try to outline the characteristic features of Charles de Foucauld's faith;

in the second his great insights; and in the third we give a selection of particularly fine texts, typical of his deep single-mindedness in the service of his God. Finally we append a short biography with indications of Charles de Foucauld's main writings.

# PART ONE

## *The Faith of Brother Charles*

Charles de Foucauld lost his faith quite early on, in his adolescence. Whatever the causes – and they were many, very similar to those which lead adolescents to challenge religion today – he eventually reached that stage at which, in his own words, 'faith was quite dead'.

On 14 August 1901, he wrote to Henry de Castries: 'For twelve years I lived without any faith whatever: nothing seemed to me to be sufficiently proven: the same level of faith which inspired so many different religions merely went to show that all of them were futile (...) I was twelve years believing and denying nothing, despairing of the truth, and not even believing in God, as I was convinced by none of the proofs for his existence.'[3]

However, during his exploration in Morocco, he had come to know groups of Jews and Muslims who were profoundly religious, and he had left Morocco with a vivid respect for those who believe, and more than a little shaken in his scepticism. He wrote: 'Islam shook me deeply . . . seeing such faith, seeing people living in the continual presence of God, I came to glimpse something bigger and more real than worldly occupations.'[4]

Islam declares to the world that faith is a submission of the mind.

But Charles de Foucauld continued to look for faith as one looks for evidence of proofs.

Suddenly one day he saw the light, and he not only

believed, but gave himself totally to the God he believed in. 'As soon as I believed there was a God, I saw that the only course open to me was to devote myself entirely to Him; my religious vocation dates from the same moment as my faith.'[5]

How had this living water welled up? Can we trace the secret workings of grace up to the moment when the gift of faith flooded into his heart?

In the letter from which we have just quoted, and in a meditation written at Nazareth in the November of 1897, Charles de Foucauld tells how he recovered his faith.[6] From these well-known passages, here is part of the meditation;

'By the sheer force of events, You pressed chastity on me, and in no time at all, that winter's end in 1886, when I had returned to my family in Paris, it became my joy and the craving of my heart (...) This was to prepare me to receive the truth (...) You inspired me with a love of virtue, pagan virtue, You let me comb the books of pagan philosophers and find nothing but emptiness and disgust . . . And then by Your grace I chanced on a Christian book[7] and felt its warmth and beauty . . . You encouraged me to feel that there I might perhaps find if not truth (I did not believe men could know the truth), at least instruction in the paths of virtue, and you inspired me to look for it, still pagan, in Christian books . . . In this way You familiarised me with the mysteries of religion . . . More and more You tightened the links that bound me to radiant souls; You had led me back into that family of mine to whom I had been so passionately attached in my childhood years . . . I recovered my former admiration for these people, and You inspired them to receive me back like the prodigal son just as if I had never wandered from

16

the paternal home (...) At the beginning of October 1886, after six months of family life, I admired virtue, I wanted it, but I still did not know you ... By what prodigies of invention, O God of all goodness, did you help me to know you? (...) I felt a need for solitude, for recollection, for devotional reading; I wanted to go into Your churches, I who did not believe in You; my mind was troubled, in anguish at searching and searching for the truth; I prayed, 'My God, if you exist, help me to know you!' (...) A marvellous helper you had,[8] who worked in silence, with gentleness, goodness and deep holiness (...) You drew me to virtue by the beauty of her soul in which virtue had never seemed to me to be more beautiful (...) You drew me to the truth by the beauty of her soul.

And then You lavished four graces on me. The first was an inspired thought: since this person is so intelligent, the religion she believes in with such devotion cannot be the foolishness I thought. The second was another inspired thought: since religion is not foolishness, perhaps it is the home of truth which has no other on earth among religions or the philosophical systems? The third was to say to me: let us study this religion then; let us take a Catholic professor of religion, a learned priest, and see what it is about and whether we should believe it. The fourth was the incomparable grace to go to Fr Huvelin for these instructions. As I entered his confessional one day towards the end of that October, somewhere between the 27th and the 30th, I thought to myself, You have showered me with every blessing, my God (...)

I asked to be instructed: he made me kneel down and make my confession, and then go to communion at once...'[9]

Written two years after his conversion, this meditation clearly sets out its stages and the many graces he received from God : a homeward journey, but not without its stumblings and its cul-de-sacs. His fine, but as he himself says[10] 'strange' prayer, 'My God, if you exist, help me to know you!', recalls the prayer of the father of the epileptic boy : "If you can do anything, have pity on us and help us" . . . "If you can", retorted Jesus, "everything is possible for anyone who has faith." Immediately the father of the boy cried out, "I do have faith. Help the little faith I have!" (Mk 9:22–24). This nascent faith and humble confession gained the man his son's cure.

For some months, Charles de Foucauld had made no progress in prayer. He was trying to look for faith in the same way that one looks for rational certainty. 'This religion cannot be foolishness (...) perhaps it is the truth (...) Let us study this religion then; let us take a Catholic professor of religion, a learned priest, and see what it is about and whether we should believe it.'

Faith does not suddenly appear at the end of a process of rational argument, it is not the fruit of human evidence. If, from God's side, faith is a pure gift of his mercy, on man's it is the breaking of God's life into an intelligence that has opened itself under the inspiration of a humble will. Without this act of unconditional surrender, the intelligence cannot penetrate beyond its rational search, it must wait in vain for the light to come.

Fr Huvelin saw intuitively that the moment had arrived and that he must not give in to the desire for intellectual inquiry, but must encourage the act of humble confession and humble prayer for God's pardon. His penitent already had faith, but not in its fulness.

Charles de Foucauld submitted. He knelt down and made his confession. He saw a great light. Then he took communion, the Bread of Life.

We can say further that this acceptance of the faith in his intelligence, after an act of the will, was for him the spiritual experience of what John calls in his Gospel 'doing the truth': 'The man who does the truth comes out into the light' (Jn 3:21). This initial gesture was to stamp his regained faith with a vigorous, often extreme, need to translate itself into action. He was to write later, commenting on Jesus' words, 'Come and see' (Jn 1:39):

'Start by "coming", by following me, by imitating me, by putting my teaching into practice, and then you will "see", you will enjoy the light to the same extent that you have lived by my words ... "Venite et videte"; my own experience has so stamped the truth of these words on my mind, that I am writing this letter to tell you.'[11]

### LIVING AND ACTIVE FAITH

When Jesus says, 'If you know me, you know my Father, too. From this moment you know him and have seen him' (Jn 14:17), he is speaking of faith in God as of a knowledge given by the light of revelation, piercing further and further into the mystery of God and, in this life on earth, blossoming in contemplation.

And when he says, 'Anyone who follows me will not be walking in the dark; he will have the light of faith' (Jn 8:12), he is speaking of faith as of a light, at once the inspiration and guide of one's every action, that breaks in on the mind that has humbly opened itself to the gift of God.

'In this sense,' writes Brother Charles, 'the life of faith consists in thinking, speaking and acting solely on the promptings of faith in accordance with the teachings and example of Jesus; in living exclusively by the supernatural motives of faith, and in silencing all the suggestions of human reason and experience, however reasonable they may appear, as soon as they conflict not only with the dogmas of Catholic belief, but even with anything the faith asks us to think, say or do.'[12]

Faith throbbed ecstatically in the heart of Brother Charles; he was a living witness to his own definition of faith : 'the gift by which we believe to the bottom of our souls all the dogmas of religion, all the truths that religion teaches us, and therefore the whole content of Holy Scripture and all the teachings of the Gospel : in short, everything the Church proposes for our belief.'[13]

However, before outlining the great intuitions of his faith, let us just remark here that for him faith is above all 'the light of life'. His unsophisticated soul, little inclined to speculative studies but meticulous, scrupulously attentive to detail and always ready for action, received God's gift for what it is : a principle of life.

'The soul who lives by faith', he writes, 'is full of fresh thoughts, fresh tastes, fresh judgements; fresh horizons open up before him (...) Wrapped round by these new truths of which the world has no inkling, he necessarily starts on a new life which the world thinks madness. The world lies in darkest night, the man of faith basks in a brilliant splendour. The bright path he treads is unseen by men, he seems to them to be setting off into emptiness like the fool he is. . . .'[14]

We can say, then, that faith moved Brother Charles less towards the heights of mystical understanding, like some great saints of the Church, than towards the truths which are the principles of life. Christian faith, of course, is not just adhering to revealed truth : it is an encounter with God who reveals himself, and who, for the believer, becomes the light of his pilgrimage : 'anyone who follows me', says Jesus, 'will not be walking in the dark'. For Charles de Foucauld, this encounter was such that he immediately wanted to belong totally to God. With a single movement of his heart, he believed and he surrendered, so that his faith and his love never went but hand in hand. As early as 1889, less than three years after his conversion, Fr Huvelin introduced him to the Prior of Solesmes Abbey as one 'who had made religion his great love'.[15]

Reading his meditations and letters, one is struck by the fact that he is concerned less with an objective grasp of our Lord's actions and words, or even the different actions of the Christian life, than with a constant search for the 'reasons for loving'.

So, for example, meditating in our Lord's phrase, 'How happy are the poor' (Mt 5 : 3), he writes :

'We must be poor in spirit, stripped of all love and attachment for what is not God, utterly emptied of everything that is not God . . . loving nothing that is not God . . . thinking of nothing that is not God . . . desiring nothing that is not God. Stripped of ourselves and others, not looking for our own or other people's good for its own sake, but pursuing only the glory of God for His sake alone.'[16]

Thus he gives poverty a theological meaning, like the 'pure love' of St John of the Cross and many mystics; but poverty is also, for him, the determination to 'envelop everything in love', to use his own words.[17]

In this perspective, prayer becomes essentially an exercise of love. Commenting on Matthew's phrase, 'In your prayers do not babble as the pagans do' (6:7), he writes:

'In this counsel (...) You are telling us (...) that for mental prayer words are not necessary: it is enough to kneel there lovingly at your feet, contemplating Your majesty with every admiration and devotion, every desire for your glory, consolation and love, in short with every movement of our hearts that love prompts us to (...) Prayer, as St Theresa tells us, consists not in speaking a lot, but in loving a lot.'[18]

As a consequence of this inclination to turn every thought and action into a gesture of love, and to look at his whole life in that light, Brother Charles' faith was vibrant and active, impatient to do God's work. He says himself:

'God's work is faith; holiness is faith; God's will, perfection, glory, what pleases Him supremely in us, is faith ... Faith in one's heart, and faith in one's deeds together make up true, living faith.'[19]

As this text shows so clearly, for Charles de Foucauld true faith is looking at life through God's spectacles. Believing and living by faith are the same thing, because to live is to love. This explains the vigour and strength of his faith borne up by an immeasurable love. His life is full of it. Everything about him bears the stamp of it: his meditations, his resolutions, his decisions, his vigils, his work.

A meditation written by way of commentary on Jesus' words, 'Courage, my daughter, your faith has restored you to health' (Mt 9:22), gives a good summary of his thoughts on the primacy of faith in the Christian life:

'The virtue our Lord rewards, the virtue He praises, is nearly always faith. Sometimes He praises love (...) sometimes humility, but such examples are rare. It is nearly always faith which He rewards and commends. Why? ... Probably because faith is, if not the supreme virtue (charity is that), at least the most important, because it is the basis of all the others, including charity, and also because it is the rarest ... Real faith, faith which inspires all one's actions, faith in the supernatural which strips the world of its mask and reveals God in all things; which abolishes the notion of "impossible", and empties the words "anxiety", "danger" and "fear" of their meaning; which gives life calm, peace, deep joy, like a child holding its mother's hand; which detaches the soul so completely from earthly things by showing up their total lack of importance and their childishness; which bestows such confidence in prayer, the confidence of a child asking its father for something useful; the faith which shows that "apart from doing what is agreeable to God, everything is vanity" ... oh, how rare that is! ... My God, give me real faith! My God, I believe, help the little faith I have!'[20]

It follows that in the light of faith, the true believer sees everything as God sees it, stamped with the infinity of God and the nothingness of creatures; in the strength of faith, he acts as God acts, sharing in God's power and peace, and serenely detached from material things.

Charles de Foucauld often stresses unlimited filial trust – the absence of all anxiety, of all fear; the courage, the quiet determination of the true believer. He applies to himself the words of Jesus : 'If your faith were the size of a mustard seed, nothing would be impossible for you' (Mt 17:20).

Faith, which is a sharing in the knowledge which God

23

has of himself, gives the mind that receives it such a feeling for the Absolute that it becomes, in the illuminated will, a strength giving a share in the indestructible strength of God. Hence the need to go to the limit, to push the possible to its extremes; and we must remember that the possible is not as creatures see it, but as the Creator sees it: faith can move mountains (Mk 11:22–3).

For Charles de Foucauld, faith always has this quality, like well-tempered steel. This is why some of his sayings, taken in conjunction with his heroic life, reverberate with extraordinary vigour and invincible faith:

– 'Yes, Jesus is enough. Where he is, nothing is missing.'
– 'Jesus is master of the impossible.'
– 'One of the things we absolutely owe to our Lord is never to be afraid.'
– 'For the proclamation of the Holy Gospel, I am ready to go to the ends of the earth and live to the end of time.'
– 'Live as if you were to be martyred today.'

# PART TWO

*The Great Insights of his Faith*

Charles de Foucauld is not a theologian, and therefore the reader must not expect him to offer a synthesis of the Christian faith. His vocation itself is difficult to express in terms of concise, rigid logic. One must try to understand his soul in quite a different perspective, and that is why it is preferable to talk about the insights of his faith than of its content. Insight means penetrating light plunging to the roots of a truth and leaving the heart on fire. Insight follows insight, and the flame burns more brightly. But there is no mutual interdependence, no logical chain of reasoning, no intellectual synthesis. There are just fresh intuitions flooding the heart with all the freedom of the Spirit.

The wind blows wherever it pleases;
you hear its sound,
but you cannot tell where it comes from or where it is
                                                    going.
That is how it is with all who are born of the Spirit.

                                                Jn 3 :8

It is not only the Spirit who comes from we know not where and goes we know not where, but also those who are born of the Spirit, that is, those who believe and live by faith.

So the faith of Brother Charles, like his life, is scored

with great intuitions, each one of which, to him, is absolute and all-absorbing, and he opens his whole soul to it as if it were the final, definitive intuition – and also the first of them all, welcomed with all the freshness of his heart. This explains his youthful eagerness and the commanding need to push himself to the limits of endurance.

The following chapters are designed to highlight these various insights. The reader will, however, remember that each intuition could equally be the only one, expressing by itself the essence of his faith and life.

### JESUS OF NAZARETH

Charles de Foucauld rediscovered God in the sacraments of confession and the eucharist, the sacraments of Jesus Christ, in October 1886.

Then he made a pilgrimage to the Holy Land, the land of Jesus Christ, at Christmas 1888 : Bethlehem first, then a few days later Jerusalem, the Upper Room, the Mount of Olives, Calvary; and, in January 1889, Nazareth.

In the Church of Jesus Christ, one has to go through Christ to reach God. 'No one can come to the Father except through me' (Jn 14:6). But the mystery of Christ is many-sided. How does the faith of each individual saved in Jesus' name encounter the Son of God made man? What can help him to that cry of Thomas' as he touched the risen Christ's wounds: 'My Lord and my God' (Jn 20:28)?

In the mind of Charles de Foucauld, the bridge was 'Jesus of Nazareth', that is, as he says so expressively himself, 'God the worker of Nazareth'.[21] It was in this mystery that his faith reached the incarnation of the Word, and Jesus became for him 'my Beloved Brother and Lord Jesus'.

Jesus of Nazareth, for him, is Jesus in his humiliation, in his poverty and smallness and abasement, in his life of 'abjection, poverty, humble labour and obscurity'. These words occur again and again in his writings. All his life he remembered a sentence from one of Fr Huvelin's sermons : 'Jesus took the last place so often that no one has ever been able to wrest it from him.' And he himself once wrote : 'As each day goes by, I feel I want to plunge further into the deepest self-effacement, following the perfect example of our Lord.'[22]

This was how he saw Jesus of Nazareth from that January day in 1889, when for the first time he set foot in Nazareth. On 24 June 1896 he wrote to Mme de Bondy :

'I'm longing to start on that life I've been looking for for seven years, the life (...) I glimpsed, felt, as I walked through the streets of Nazareth where our Lord had trod, a poor workman lost in self-effacement and obscurity.'[23]

In similar vein he wrote on 12 April 1897, a few days after his arrival in Nazareth :

'I am settled in Nazareth . . . Here, as completely as I could possibly hope for, I have found, by God's grace, what I was looking for : poverty, solitude, self-effacement, humble work, complete obscurity, the most perfect possible imitation of the life of our Lord Jesus as he must have lived it in Nazareth . . . I have embraced the humble and obscure existence of God, the worker of Nazareth.'[24]

I believe that these words admirably express the most basic intuition of his faith in Jesus Christ, the Son of God made man : 'the humble and obscure existence of God, the worker of Nazareth'.

It translates into his own language St Paul's insight into the mystery, the fundamental humility, of Christ, as expressed in *Philippians* :

> His state was divine,
> yet he did not cling
> to his equality with God
> but emptied himself
> to assume the condition of a slave,
> and became as men are.
>
> 2 : 6–7

'The incarnation', writes Charles de Foucauld, 'has its source in the goodness of God . . . The first thing to strike us is so marvellous, so astonishing, that it shines out like some dazzling unmistakeable signpost : the infinite humility contained in such a mystery . . . God, Being, the Infinite, the Perfect, the Creator, the Almighty, immense and sovereign Lord of all becoming man (...) and appearing on earth like a man, the least of men.'[25]

Is it legitimate, is it the fruit of an objective reading of the Gospel, to see Jesus, whether it be in the manger, during his thirty hidden years at Nazareth, on the roads of Galilee and Judaea, or on the cross, solely in terms of humility, poverty, abandonment, abjection, solitude, suffering, contempt?

Faith is not a light of reason, it stabs straight to the heart of the mystery, and with the intuitive knowledge it gains it sheds a brilliant light on the mystery as a whole. It seems to simplify, but it is divine wisdom and the language of the very Spirit of God.

St Paul, writing to the Corinthians, says that the only knowledge he claimed was about 'Jesus, and only about him as the crucified Christ' (1 Co 2:2).

The prophet Isaiah, long before Paul, expressed the same view. He said of the 'Suffering Servant' that he was

> without beauty, without majesty,
> no looks to attract our eyes;
> a thing despised and rejected by men,
> a man of sorrows and familiar with suffering,
> a man to make people screen their faces.
>
> Is 53:3

And Ps 22, from which Christ quoted the opening words as he hung on the cross, calls him

> now more worm than man,
> scorn of mankind, jest of the people.
>
> Ps 22:6

Is it not the extreme limit of abjection that while he was the only begotten Son of God he was put to death by crucifixion?

It is easy to see why the great spiritual writers, like the prophets and the apostles, cast the whole human life of Christ in this light which dazzles the eye and makes the onlooker 'weep with sorrow and love'.[26]

## JESUS CHRIST IN THE EUCHARIST

'I have returned to my cloister, at the foot of the divine Tabernacle, in full view of the Beloved, to lead a life as much like the life of the divine home at Nazareth as my barren heart will allow.'[27]

This text, written at Beni-Abbès on 8 April 1905, but which he could have written at any time between 4 March 1897 (his arrival at Nazareth) and 1 December 1916 (his death at Tamanrasset at the hands of Senousis ruffians), shows us Brother Charles of Jesus living day and night in the presence of the Blessed Sacrament just as if he were living in the holy house of Nazareth with Mary and Joseph, constantly surveyed by Jesus.

There is a realism about his faith, just as if, living in the Holy Land, he were in the tangible presence of Jesus. With this same gift of imagining himself in one of the places he touched, venerated, kissed because Jesus had sanctified them in his mortal life, he wrote from Nazareth to his friend Fr Jérôme :

'It's still Christmastide; in body I'm at Nazareth (...) but in mind I've been at Bethlehem for a month, and it's from there, beside the crib, between Mary and Joseph, that I'm writing this letter. The weather's perfect : outside it's cold and it's snowing – images of the world; but in the cave, lit up by Jesus' presence, it's as cosy as could be : quiet, warm and bright! Our much loved Fr Abbot has asked me what the Child Jesus has been whispering to me for a month as I watch at His feet at night, between His Holy Parents, when He comes to my arms and into my heart at Holy Communion. Well, He says over and over again, "We must do God's will, God's will".'[28]

He does not analyse, as a theologian would, the nature of the Real Presence; he is not at all concerned to be theologically exact in his language when he talks about the signs of the eucharist. It is enough for him, in his all-consuming desire to love, if he believes :

32

'The Holy Eucharist is Jesus, all Jesus! . . . In the Holy Eucharist You are there, my beloved Jesus, living and whole, as fully as you were in the home of the Holy Family at Nazareth (...) Oh, let us never leave the presence of the Holy Eucharist for a single moment as long as Jesus allows us to be there.'[29]

In this faith of his in the eucharist, Charles de Foucauld is no more mistaken than the Curé of Ars, who in tears at the altar clasped the consecrated host and said, 'Jesus, if I knew I was not going to see you in heaven, I should never let you go now.'

'The Eucharist is Jesus, present on our altars "always, yes, to the end of time", the true Emmanuel, "God with us", at all times and everywhere on earth exposed to our gaze, our adoration and our love, and by means of this perpetual presence transforming the night of our lives into a lustrous splendour.'[30]

For Charles de Foucauld, then, the eucharist is so real a presence of Jesus in the tabernacle that it brightens the whole land and becomes the source of sanctification and salvation for all the people round it, just as Jesus' silent and hidden presence at Nazareth was a source of grace for his fellow-villagers.

It is this presence of Jesus that Charles de Foucauld wishes to be with him always, in the solitude of the desert, that he wishes to spread wherever he goes, whether he is pitching a tent or building a hut, a hermitage or a fraternity. In this way he will always be 'in the house of Nazareth where, between Mary and Joseph, he is clasped like a little brother by his elder Brother Jesus, present night and day in the Sacred Host'.[31]

This is like the simple and innocent language of a child,

33

but the faith behind it is the faith of a man who could live alone in the desert for fifteen years, a faithful worshipper by night and by day in the presence of God.

The eucharist is also the Bread of Life. For Charles de Foucauld it was truly his 'daily bread', from the day when he received at communion the gift of living faith and of which he said, in the realistic thoughts of St John Chrysostom whom he read a great deal:

'In Holy Communion, God comes to us in a bodily way; our mouths touch the Body of our Lord as our Lady's lips did.'[32]

Finally, the eucharist is the Holy Sacrifice of the Mass, in which the immolated Jesus 'offers himself as a sacrifice to his Father'. To offer this sacrifice and in so doing give the greatest possible glory to God, Charles expressed a wish, from April 1900 onwards, to be ordained priest. For a long time he had rejected the idea so as to be able to remain for always in the humility and self-effacement of the life of Nazareth, but, as he wrote himself:

'Never does a man imitate our Lord more perfectly than when he is offering the Holy Sacrifice . . . I must be humble where our Lord was humble, practise humility as He practised it, and so practise it in the priesthood as he did.'[33]

It is slightly disconcerting to follow his thoughts, which proceed not by keener analysis or deeper understanding of the dogma, but by a contemplative approach to the mystery of the imitation of Christ. He wants to be 'a priest like Jesus'. But having seen 'the priesthood of Jesus, in the last moments of his life, from the Last Supper to his last sigh', he wrote these words, which explain so beautifully the eucharistic freshness of his life:

34

'Priests at the altar must sacrifice to Jesus' Father, for his glory and the salvation of men in the Holy Sacrifice, as Jesus offered himself at the Last Supper; and on their cross they must offer themselves with Jesus to His Father, for His glory, the glory of Jesus and the salvation of men, suffering with Jesus the agony, passion and death, to the extent that Jesus is pleased to invite them to share his chalice and be victims with Him.'[34]

Offering the Sacrifice of the Mass, Charles de Foucauld entered more deeply into an understanding of the eucharistic mystery, and prepared himself for that invitation which in fact Jesus willed to offer him on the evening of 1 December 1916.

### THE HAPPINESS OF GOD

'The happiness of God', the unchangeable happiness of the 'Beloved' : these words recur frequently in his meditations and letters.

It is quite certain that he himself experienced it as a direct consequence of his love for Jesus. From the Trappist monastery of Akbes he wrote to Marie de Bondy :

'However sad I am when I kneel at the foot of the altar and say to our Lord Jesus, "Lord, you are infinitely happy and lack nothing", I cannot help adding : I'm happy, too, and I lack nothing. Your happiness is enough for me . . . This is true, it must be like that if we love our Lord.'[35]

Charles of Jesus does not analyse this infinite happiness of the Lord he loves. It is a simple conviction of his faith, an intuition of his heart : his Beloved is beyond

35

suffering now, he has risen, he is in the glory of God. Developing this thought, he wrote during his retreat in November 1897 at Nazareth:

'You are rising from the dead, You are ascending to heaven! . . . And I see You now in your glory! You are beyond suffering, You will never suffer again. You are happy, and will be happy for ever . . . My God, if I really love You, how happy I must be! If I am concerned above all for your glory, how satisfied, how blissful I must be! . . . My God, You are happy for Eternity, You lack nothing. You are infinitely and eternally blessed! . . . I'm blessed, too, My God, because I love You above all things. I can truly say that I lack nothing . . . that I am in seventh heaven, that whatever happens I am happy because of Your blessedness! . . .'[36]

Charles de Foucauld left everything behind him, his family, his friends, his country, for Jesus' sake, and he was there at Nazareth, where Jesus had lived. Jesus, the Living God, was nearer to him than all the human beings on earth. The believer understands this. The unbeliever cannot see how personal the living God can become. Love is ecstatic: the lover is more fully present in his beloved than in himself. This is true even of human love. In his living, concrete faith, Charles wanted his love for Jesus to follow the same path.

As early as June 1897, he wrote from Nazareth laying down his guiding principle of life:

'*Your spirit*: the spirit of the love of God and forgetfulness of self, in the contemplation and joy of his happiness.'[37]

Forgetfulness of self – not only to fight the radical ego-ism from which we all suffer – but also forgetfulness of one's own poverty of spirit, the daily experience of one's weakness, and the painful awareness of one's nothingness : this is what is needed.

The Christian who has achieved self-knowledge in the light of faith does not become self-centred; he is carried totally out of himself in his admiration of God's beauty, or, as Charles de Foucauld would say in his own way of expressing the mystery, in 'his thoughts on the happiness of God'. He writes :

'A deep peace floods the soul, transitory things are nothing. We are walking towards God, contemplating His immense happiness and rejoicing for ever in the thought of the infinite, perfect, unchangeable happi-ness of this God we love; we are happy with the happiness of the Beloved, and the thought of His unchangeable peace calms the soul . . . The sight of my own nothingness does not weigh me down : it helps me forget myself and think only of Him who is all in all.'[38]

So in Charles of Jesus' soul what started as the burning determination of a heart that loves and wants to love passionately becomes an experience, a fruit of his contem-plation of God which, in keeping with his profoundest characteristics, draws him to commit himself totally in love. He loses himself in this loving repose more even than in his impassioned gaze into the depths of the mystery. He is overwhelmed by God's peace.

Beni-Abbès, Monday of Holy Week 1903. 'The more the soul forgets itself and enjoys the delights of Jesus' happiness, the more it experiences that peace of which it is said, "Happy the peacemakers".'[39]

Amra (a little to the north of Idelès), 15 July 1904. 'All is sweetness for me, dear friend, I view all things in the light of God's immense peace, infinite happiness, and the unchangeable glory of the Blessed and ever-peaceful Trinity . . . Everything is absorbed into the happiness of knowing that God is God.'[40]

### SHOUTING THE GOSPEL FROM THE HOUSETOP OF ONE'S LIFE

When we talk about the Gospel in the life of Brother Charles, we are immediately led to think of his imitation of Christ, because for him the Gospel is not merely the book which gives him knowledge of the Lord he adores, it is also the *only model* he is to imitate exclusively: 'Read the Scriptures . . . and follow Me, Me alone.'[41]

There is in Brother Charles one combined movement of knowledge and love expressing itself in imitation. Where there is no imitation, there can be no love, and no knowledge either. The Gospel is not simply a book, one among many: it is God's fruitful word, sharper than any two-edged sword, transforming and moulding on the pattern of Jesus, who said: 'If you make my word your home, you will indeed be my disciples, you will learn the truth, and the truth will make you free' (Jn 8:31). Is this not the same as saying that to reach a knowledge of the truth, one must make Jesus' word one's home and keep it, that is, carry out the Master's commandments and follow him as a disciple?

Then whoever keeps his word becomes the dwelling-place of God's word, the incarnate Word Jesus, and he 'lives the Gospel', in Brother Charles' own phrase. 'We must go back to the Gospel. If we do not live it, Jesus will not live in us.'[42]

Brother Charles does not read the Gospel for lofty ideas, or an ideal of the perfect human life, or the guide-lines and dialectic for the transformation of society. He wishes rather

'to be impregnated with the Spirit of Jesus, ceaselessly reading and re-reading, meditating and re-meditating his words and example: so that they become in his soul as it were a drop of water falling and falling on to the same spot of a paving-stone.'[43]

The Gospel, then, reveals a living Person to him, Jesus his Master, 'his only Master because only He is perfectly holy.'[44] He is not looking for an abstract ideal of virtue, a perfect blueprint: he is seeking to imitate Jesus, because

' "perfection means being like the Master". It is foolish, in fact sinful, to imagine that one can be more perfect than He on even the tiniest point: "Who is like God?" We must not strive to be greater than Jesus in men's eyes . . . Our Master was despised, the servant must not be honoured; the Master was poor, the servant must not be rich; the Master lived by the work of His hands, the servant must not live idly; the Master went about on foot, the servants should not go on horseback; the Master made the little ones, the poor, the workers His friends, the servant must not fraternise with the rich; the Master passed for a worker, the servant must not pass for a notability; the Master was calumniated, the servant must not be thought highly of; the Master was ill-clothed, ill-nourished and badly housed, the servant must not be well-clothed, well-nourished and well-housed; the Master worked and was tired, the servant must not rest; the Master wanted to be small. the servant must not strive to be great.'[45]

This text, typical of his meditation on the Gospel, shows that when Brother Charles talks about the imitation of Jesus, he is not referring simply to an interior imitation of his virtues, or a conformity of one's soul to his; no, he means as perfect an imitation as possible of Jesus' whole life, his actions, his state, his work and labours, his sufferings and his griefs.[46]

He wants to tread where he has trodden, to 'follow Him as closely as possible', and even more 'to share' : 'I cannot imagine a love which does not feel the *need*, an *imperious need*, to conform with, to resemble, and above all to share all the troubles, difficulties and labours of life....'[47]

The saints do not regard Jesus as having lived once upon a time; for them he is alive now, and they want to live with him and share his life.

Jesus' life spins itself out in front of their very eyes, from the crib to the cross, and Brother Charles is there with him, poor and humble, praying and fasting, working with his hands at 'the humble work of Jesus', as he puts it. He started at Nazareth, because Jesus spent thirty years there. 'For thirty years You lived the life of a poor workman in this very Nazareth I have the great joy to be in now, where I have the unutterable, the inexpressibly profound happiness of raking manure....'[48]

This is the language of a man who has left everything behind, seeing the world as a place of vanity, false joys and empty grandeur; a man who has discovered that God became small.

'My Lord Jesus, Your faithful disciple, loving You with all his heart, and loath to see himself richer than his Master, will lose no time in becoming quite poor.'[49]

It was at Nazareth, his eyes fixed immovably on Jesus

in solitude and intimate communion with his Beloved, that Brother Charles understood what God's will is: 'to be where God wants us to be, to do what God expects of us, and in whatever state God wishes us to be, to think, speak and act as Jesus would have thought, spoken and acted if His Father had willed Him in that state'.[50]

This explains how Charles de Foucauld could take the lowest place with Jesus at Nazareth, 'immeasurably poor', and then go on to want to follow him in everything, not only because 'imitation gives the measure of one's love', but because Jesus left Nazareth to announce the Gospel. His life, however, was to be always and everywhere a life of Nazareth. 'May I live in Nazareth everywhere, hidden with Jesus.'

How can we explain these continual references to Nazareth, right up to the end of his life, even when he had left the Poor Clares, where he had been employed as a member of the domestic staff, and had become an apostle of the Gospel ready to go to the ends of the earth?

The reason is that the mystery of Nazareth was the initial light in which he came to know the Lord Jesus, and it was to remain with him from then on. Whatever he did or was led to do by his extreme love for Jesus, his Master, and by a desire to do as much good as he could for men, he was stamped with the seal of Nazareth.

How can we define this seal, this light, of Nazareth?

Firstly, it is the state of poverty, lowliness, abandonment, littleness, in which one is the butt of men's contempt and indifference.

And secondly, it includes the evangelical virtues, humility, gentleness, 'being one who serves', the desire of suffering; the need to be where 'there is extreme privation' of God, with those who suffer most from sickness and deprivation in hot countries.

In short, it means to be the universal brother, espec-

ially the brother of the poorest, the friend of those who
have no friends.

This is what Brother Charles calls 'shouting the Gospel
from the housetop of one's life'.

### THE GOSPEL PHRASE WHICH TRANSFORMED MY LIFE

On 1 August 1916, four months before his death, he
wrote to Louis Massignon from Tamanrasset:

> 'I do not think there is a Gospel phrase which has
> made a deeper impression on me and transformed my
> life more than this one: "Insofar as you did this to one
> of the least of these brothers of mine, you did it to me."
> One has only to think that these words were spoken
> by the uncreated Truth, who also said, "This is my
> body . . . this is my blood . . ." to be kindled into search-
> ing for Jesus and loving Him in the "least of these
> brothers of mine", these sinners, these poor people.'[51]

The remarkable point about this text is not so much
the mention of the second commandment, 'which is like
the first', but the reference to the eucharist. His faith led
him to see under the consecrated species of bread and
wine the Body and Blood of Jesus; similarly he saw in
every human being, 'behind the veils and appearances,
an unspeakably holy being, a member, a portion, of the
Body of our beloved Jesus'.[52]

It is in such dense, realistic language, in which we catch
an echo of St John Chrysostom, that Charles de Foucauld
translates his faith in Christ's mystical Body. All men, for
different reasons, are members of the Body of Christ, because by his incarnation Christ became eminently one
of them. Jesus is not in any way exclusive, either for the

42

rich or for the poor, because they were all created in the image of God; but he had a preference for the poor.

In 1899, when he was at Nazareth, he wrote the constitutions and rule for his projected foundation of the Little Brothers of the Sacred Heart. In one passage he describes the universal charity he would like to see characteristic of the Fraternity:

'The Little Brothers will not only gladly welcome the guests, the poor, the sick who ask for hospitality; they will invite in those whom they encounter, begging them, kneeling if necessary like Abraham to the angels, not to "pass your servants by" without accepting their hospitality, their attentions, their marks of brotherly love. Everyone in the neighbourhood must know that the Fraternity is the house of God where every poor or sick person is always invited, called, wanted, welcomed with joy and gratitude by brothers who love and cherish them and regard their entry as the discovery of a great treasure. They are in fact the greatest treasure of all, Jesus himself: Insofar as you do this to one of the least of these brothers of mine, you do it to me.'[53]

This is what he himself practised at Beni-Abbès.

'I want to accustom all the inhabitants, Christians, muslims, Jews and non-believers, to look on me as their brother, the universal brother. Already they're calling this house "the fraternity" (khaoua in Arabic) – about which I'm delighted'[54] – 'and realising that the poor have a brother here – not only the poor, though: all men.'[55]

Charles de Foucauld, who calls the Lord Jesus his Beloved Brother, his elder Brother, wants all men, who are all members of Jesus, to regard him as their brother. The same fraternal blood unites all men : not only the human blood from Adam, but the blood of Christ, Son of God made man.

Both at Beni-Abbès in 1902, and later in the Hoggar in 1905, the first distress to draw his compassion was the miserable life of the slaves.

He wanted immediate action. He wrote to his bishop Mgr Guérin : 'It seems to me to be beside the point to launch into a detailed account of the ill-treatment suffered by the slaves in the Sahara and the oases. They are ill-treated, it is true, but even if they were well treated, the biggest evil, the biggest injustice of all would remain : that they are slaves.'[56]

Others have been affronted by slavery, which is one of the most shameful and immoral forms of the oppression and exploitation of man by man. To this very day there are forms of oppression which are equally unjust. But besides this mental and emotional revolt, Charles de Foucauld also experienced the painful dictates of his Christian faith.

To a friend who had advised him to be patient and prudent, he replied :

'Far be it from me to want to speak and write; but I cannot betray *my children*, and fail to do for JESUS, living in his members, what He needs : it is JESUS in this deplorable condition.'[57]

In the man who suffers, who is oppressed, who is a slave, Charles de Foucauld's faith sees Jesus who suffers, who is oppressed, who is a slave.

What would happen in the world if all Christians had this same faith and these same views?

44

Charles de Foucauld left for the Carthusians, then for Nazareth, because to his mind, since the first commandment is to love God with all one's heart, everything must be embraced in love, and love pushes one to the perfect imitation of the Beloved. In his continual meditation of the Gospel and in his eucharistic contemplation, he discovered that Jesus loved us by suffering for us. What struck him above all in Christ's suffering was the immense love for us it reveals.

'My God, You suffered all that for love, for love of us, to make us holy, to urge us to love You at the sight of your immense love (...) You did not suffer so much, Jesus, in order to redeem us: the least of your actions is of infinite worth, because it is the action of God, and would have been abundantly sufficient to redeem a thousand worlds (...) It was to make us holy, to prompt us, to draw us, to love You freely, because there is no more powerful way of attracting love than by loving.'

It follows for the disciple of Jesus that

'we cannot possibly love Him without imitating Him (...) Since He suffered and died in agony, we cannot love Him and yet want to be crowned with roses while He was crowned with thorns . . . We must love Him just as He loved us, in the very same way.'[58]

His one desire was to share Jesus' suffering, to be like him and give him proof of his love.

Then the mystery of Jesus the Saviour came increasingly to occupy his thoughts. Jesus' sufferings in his pas-

45

sion and death on the cross were the suffering and death of the divine Lamb, offered in sacrifice 'for the redemption of many'. And he adds:

'May we, like You, be "victims for the redemption of many", as we unite our prayers to Yours, and our sufferings to Yours, following your example, we mortify ourselves to make our own small contribution to Your work of redemption.'[59]

Very quickly he began to see the whole of Jesus' life in the light of the redemption. Jesus, whose name means Saviour, began the work of men's salvation from the first moment of his life on earth, by the acceptance of poverty, self-effacement and suffering from his birth, his prayer and penance at Nazareth, and finally his work of evangelisation with all its fatigues and disappointments, physical and moral sufferings, persecution and hostility, ending in the passion, the cross, and death.[60]

This contemplation of Jesus as Saviour led Charles de Foucauld to accept the priesthood to be able to take the Bread of Life to the poor, to the most deeply suffering; he wanted to be a priest like Jesus, to minister to the 'sheep without a shepherd'.[61]

The last fifteen years of his life make no sense unless they are seen as the expression of his faithful discipleship of Jesus in Jesus' work for the salvation of men, not excluding the ultimate, the supreme sacrifice.

From texts written at Beni-Abbès and Tamanrasset, the latter dating from between January and June 1916, one can elaborate this programme of life:

– I have come to bring fire ...
– To save what was lost ...
– Jesus wanted his name, Saviour, to express his life's

work : the salvation of souls; in imitation of the Unique Model, our life's work too must be the salvation of souls.

– To see in every human being someone to be saved.
– In order to achieve this, one must be all things to all men with one consuming desire : to give souls to Jesus.
– To put the good of souls before every other consideration . . . .
– To offer the Holy Sacrifice perfectly . . .
– To adore as much as possible, to be good to all . . .
– To pray and do penance for all men.

Beyond the restricted circle of the desert villages Beni-Abbès and Tamanrasset and the sparse Sahara population, Charles de Foucauld's faith looked to the salvation of all men. As early as his Nazareth retreat resolutions, he commented :

'One must have zeal for souls, a burning love for the salvation of men who have all been redeemed at unique cost. One is to despise nobody, *but desire the greatest good of all men*, since they are all cloaked with Jesus' blood . . . I resolve *to do all I possibly can for the salvation of all souls*, according to the conditions of my state, since they were all so dearly bought by Jesus and loved by him.'[62]

A few months before his death, he wrote from Tamanrasset :

'The Holy Martyrs of Japan. Let us pray for the conversion of Japan, and work there if possible.'

To save souls 'redeemed at unique cost', what, again, did he intend to do?

Well, there was the Word, and the determination to

47

do everything in his power to help those around him, and especially to make increasingly his own the humiliations of Christ. The vision never falters.

'Put the Gospel into practice, in abjection and poverty.'[63] 'If I could, only I can't, do otherwise than lose myself totally in union with His divine will, I should prefer total failure and perpetual solitude. In this way I should have a share in the humiliations and cross of our divine Beloved whom I have always wished to serve above all.'[64]

'It was at the moment of his supreme humiliation that Jesus saved the world.' This phrase of St John of the Cross' was often on Brother Charles' lips, and on the very day of his death, 1 December 1916, he wrote it in a letter to M. Massignon.

In his view it commented so aptly on Jesus' words: Unless a wheat grain falls on the ground and dies, it remains only a single grain; but if it dies, it yields a rich harvest (Jn 12 : 24).

'Jesus saved the world by his cross; by the cross we must continue the work of redemption to the end of time, letting Jesus live in us and make up all that has still to be undergone by Christ. Without the cross there can be no union with the crucified Jesus, no union with Jesus the Saviour.'

This passage comes from the *Directoire* addressed to Christians who wish to consecrate their lives in the world to extending Jesus' kingdom.[65]

48

The reader is constantly meeting such words as poverty, self-effacement, suffering, self-denial, in Brother Charles' writings. A question comes to mind : does this not betray a rather morbid picture of the Christian life, a sort of fixation with pain and sorrow?

Well, one may remark in the first place that a great many of Brother Charles' writings were written for his own encouragement : personal meditations, retreat resolutions, examinations of conscience and the like. Secondly, it may be readily admitted that he took his love to the extreme, and as a consequence drew his bow almost to breaking point.

That said, however, our account of Brother Charles would be incomplete if it did not state quite categorically that he was happy. This is true not only when he was directly experiencing the Lord's consolations, when he felt the Lord's presence with its immense peace and the joy of being loved and of loving in return : 'The sweetness and peace are so exquisite, so divine, when the soul is immersed in the pure love of Jesus' heart.'[66]

No, he was always happy, because he had discovered a living spring, a water of life welling up for ever : the imitation of Jesus, to do as he did, to be like him. There can be no greater joy for the disciple than to be like his Master. 'Everything which makes us more like the Beloved draws us closer to Him and gives us perfect happiness.'[67]

He imitates Jesus in his prayer, in his fasting, in his poverty and littleness and manual work. His house is just like the house of the Holy Family at Nazareth. On 4 December 1912, he wrote to a friend: 'With its forty impoverished farm-workers, Tamanrasset is just as Nazareth and Bethlehem could have been in our Lord's time.'[68]

The heart that loves has the great gift of finding traces of the Beloved everywhere. Charles de Foucauld was a man who thought, reflected and acted with insight, energy and precision in everything he undertook. His gaze went beyond the merely visible, and his faith had a simplicity about it which made him see everything 'in a heavenly light, beautiful with the beauty of God himself'.[69]

All the events of his life, important and unimportant alike, reminded him of Jesus and took him further into Jesus. The coin of all he saw was stamped with the head of Christ. Such a view of things led him to some marvellously fresh and tender thoughts:

> 'My ideal', he said, 'is to go on foot without luggage and to work with my hands, just as Jesus did at Nazareth;[70]
> 'to minister to the sick and the poor (...) as Jesus did when he washed his disciples' feet;[71]
> 'to give more to my guests than to myself (...) because Jesus is in them all: barley-bread for me, wheat-bread for Jesus;[72]
> 'to be robbed willingly: to commit the little I have, like Jesus, to thieves...'

What faith, what an excess of love in these words! What an extreme desire to be like the One so passionately loved!

One is not in the least surprised that just as Brother Charles refers to his 'keeping in step with Jesus', he also talks about 'Jesus keeping in step with him'.

When he arrived in the Hoggar district of Algeria with a view to settling there, he built a hut of earth and stone at Tamanrasset. This was in August 1905. The hut had two rooms, each less than five by eight feet.

On 26 August of that same year, he wrote to a friend:

'Pray that I remain faithful to the divine Jesus, who has made himself small enough to keep me company in this tiny house, even tinier than the house of Nazareth.'[73]


## EVERYTHING THAT UNITES US TO THE CHURCH UNITES US TO JESUS

In my opinion these words,[74] written at Nazareth, perfectly sum up Brother Charles' faith in the Church.

When the mystery of the Church was brought before him once more as he received absolution from Fr Huvelin, it was at once connected in his mind with the mystery of Christian obedience, that is, the Christian's obligation to look for God's will in obedience to the Church. To Charles de Foucauld, a man all of a piece, energetic and indomitable, quite capable of doing on his own things never before done, it was imperative, once by grace he had turned back to God, to opt for obedience to the Church, the representative of God. If he had not, to what excesses of mortification might he not have succumbed? The story of his life demonstrates beyond any doubt how wholeheartedly, in his passionate search for God's will, he submitted, in avenues trod by none before him.

It could not have been easy for him. Constantly he had to remind himself of Jesus' words to his apostles: 'Anyone who listens to you listens to me' (Lk 10:16).

From Beni-Abbès he wrote to Fr Huvelin, on 13 December 1903, when he was beginning to wonder whether he should not move further south, asking him to 'write or telegraph (Beni-Abbès, via Beni-Ounif, South Oranais, Algeria) and I shall obey you : "Anyone who listens to you listens to me".'[75]

What obedience! and what impatience: he had not been at Beni-Abbès two years! In his letter he made sure his own views were clear: 'My own feeling is quite definitely that I should leave on 10 January.'[76]

Charles de Foucauld was a man of action, and he was consumed with a burning fire. Nevertheless he obeyed like a child, in imitation of a God who became obedient, from his birth to his cross. He imagined Jesus speaking to him :

'How perfectly My life at Nazareth (...) was a sermon on *obedience*. I who was God submitted for thirty years to My parents, saints no doubt, but nonetheless human, and I am God! . . . How could you, seeing Me so obedient to those to whom I owed no obedience, whose sovereign Lord, Creator and Judge I was, refuse a *perfect obedience* to your lawful superiors: "Anyone who listens to them", I say, "listens to me".'[77]

We may note that although he saw in all Christ's human life the reflexion of 'the Man of Sorrows', he also saw the reflexion of the Creator's divine glory. His vision prescinds from time. When he wrote that Christ was 'so obedient to those to whom (he) owed no obedience', we should not look for a precise theological statement on the incarnation.

The mystery of the Church is also the mystery of Christ's mystical Body which is composed of all his living members.

Charles de Foucauld's main thought is for the whole Church in its length, breadth and depth, and his concern is to become a more and more intimate part of it, at one with all the children of God, with all 'whom the Spirit of God animates', and he adds, quoting St Paul, with creation itself hoping to be 'freed, like us, from its slavery to decadence, to enjoy the same freedom and glory as the children of God' (Rm 8 : 21).

It was in this ardent wish to be at one with the Church that Charles de Foucauld discovered the prime calling of creation and the Church : adoration and thanksgiving, praise and love.

It was with such thoughts as these that he recited the Divine Office, the prayer of the Church, of 'the beloved Church, the Bride of Christ' in its three parts : militant, suffering and triumphant.[78]

His particular image to describe the Church on earth was that of the Spouse of the crucified Christ, because to his mind the Church's task is to continue Christ's work, the redemption of the world, after his death. This task cannot be achieved without the cross.

'The royal way of the Cross is the only one for the elect, for the Church, for each individual disciple; it is a law to the end of time : the Church and souls, spouses of the crucified Groom, must share His thorns and carry the Cross with Him. The law of love is that the spouse should want above all else to share the life of the Groom.'[79]

Jesus' words on the effectiveness of any ministry or apostolate apply equally to the Church as to each one of its members : 'Unless a wheat grain falls on the ground and dies, it remains only a single grain; but if it dies, it yields a rich harvest' (Jn 12 : 24). 'As St John of the Cross observes, it was at the moment of His supreme humiliation, at the very moment of His death, that Jesus (...) saved the world.'[80]

53

There is a faith here, and a perfect hope, which are not conducive to a resigned acceptance of failure or a natural shyness and prudence, but which presuppose that the Church, ever faithful to its mission of preaching the Gospel to all creatures, has constantly before its mind those words of Jesus': 'I have come to bring fire to the earth, and how I wish it were blazing already! There is a baptism I must still receive, and how great is my distress till it is over!' (Lk 12 :49–50).

For Charles of Jesus it would be intolerable for the Church to show fear, timidity or prudence. He wrote to Mgr Guérin, Apostolic Prefect for the Sahara, who had advised him to be prudent in any action he might take in favour of the slaves :

'The reasons you are kind enough to offer and which must carry so much weight with me, not only because they come from you but also because their intrinsic good sense is incontestable, nevertheless cause me some un-ease in that the representatives of Jesus seem happy to defend "in secret" (and not "from the housetops") a cause of such justice and charity. I say this only because the child should have no secrets from its father, but should express itself with total confidence and frankness.'[81]

With humility like this saints have often recalled the Church to its mission.

### OUR LADY AND THE SAINTS

Charles de Foucauld had a great devotion to the saints, but in his own way. His unique love was for Jesus, the unique model, and he could be no one else's disciple.

He was fond of reading the writings of the saints, especially St John Chrysostom, St Theresa of Avila and St John of the Cross. They all had a strong influence on his thinking. But as he himself said, 'We must concentrate on the Gospel. That is what we shall be judged on . . . not this or that book, this or that spiritual master, this or that teacher, this or that saint.'[82]

He also read the lives of the saints, because they were 'a sort of commentary on the Gospel'. His conclusion was that we should 'look to the saints, but not spend too much time at it. We should rather, with them, contemplate Jesus whom they themselves spent their whole lives contemplating (...) taking from each life what seems to us to be most in line with our Lord's teaching and example, for he is our only true model. We can learn from them, certainly, but this must be not to imitate *them*, but to be able to imitate *Jesus* better.'[83]

This is an example of Jesus' words: 'You have only one Master . . . only one Teacher, the Christ' (Mt 23:8–11). It is also an example of the sovereign freedom exercised by the Christian who has only one love.

It is necessary to bear this in mind if we are to understand the place of the saints in his life. Such a conclusion was not the fruit of a theological reflexion on Christ's unique mediation; it was the fruit of a vision of faith and of a steady meditation on the Gospel. He imagines Jesus' saying, 'Follow Me, Me only . . . Do not come to Bethany to see Me *and* Lazarus; come to see Me only.'[84]

A second point must be made, too.

The saints he had the greatest affection for, the saints he lived with in his solitude, from his return to the Holy Land, were the saints mentioned in the Gospel who lived with Jesus during his earthly life. The reason for this is that in his vivid faith and burning love, Brother Charles became Jesus' contemporary. He did not live in the past;

his life was 'a life with Jesus', as if Jesus had never left the earth. This is a perfectly legitimate idea, because since the advent of the Son of God made man, the earth holds a divine presence.

At Beni-Abbès he wrote: 'I am in the house at Nazareth, where, between Mary and Joseph, I am *clasped like a little brother* by his elder Brother Jesus, present day and night in the Sacred Host.'[85]

From Tamanrasset, on 16 December 1905, he wrote: 'Don't worry about my being alone, without friends or spiritual help. Far from suffering from my solitude, I love it. I have the Blessed Sacrament, the best of friends, and I talk to him day and night; I have the Blessed Virgin and St Joseph, and all the saints.'[86]

Peopling his solitude, the saints of the Gospel are his invisible daily companions.

First and foremost of these is our Lady, whom he calls his mother, because he is Jesus' 'little brother'. From the annunciation to the cross, depending on the liturgical period or his own meditations, or his occupations and the events of his life,[87] he wanted to love her as Jesus did, and to do everything Jesus did for her. He became a part of the Holy Family; and the people of Nazareth looked on him, too, as 'the worker, the son of Mary'.

On 8 May 1899, he wrote to Mme de Bondy[88] that he was 'returning to his life as "the worker, the son of Mary" ' – what an evocative phrase, expressing his close identification with his Beloved Brother Jesus.

The life of the Holy Family carries on, and he lives through the various events as if they were part of the events of his own life. For example, he wrote from Tamanrasset on 9 June 1908:

'I have two hermitages nearly a thousand miles apart! I spend three months at the one in the north, six

56

months in the one in the south, and each year I set aside three months to go from one to the other. When I am in one of my hermitages, I live a cloistered life, trying to live a life of work and prayer, a life of Nazareth. When I travel, I think of the flight into Egypt, and of the Holy Family's annual pilgrimage to Jerusalem.'[89]

After our Lady and St Joseph the head of the Holy Family, he had a special devotion for John the Baptist, the apostles, the holy women, especially Mary Magdalene, whom he identified, as was usual then, with Mary of Bethany, the sister of Martha and Lazarus.[90]

So all Jesus' friends became his. He read the Gospel with them; he contemplated and listened to his Lord with them; he adored, gave praise, shared in his sufferings and joys, all with them. And when he prays to them, it is to ask their help in loving the unique Beloved more.

At the beginning of his Gospel meditations, written while he was a Trappist at Akbes monastery in Asia Minor, he writes:

'Mother, St Mary Magdalene, St Joseph, St John the Baptist, St Peter, St Paul, my guardian angel, you holy women who prepared spices for our Lord's burial, prepare this work of mine, prepare me, and pour me out as a sweet-smelling perfume at our Lord's feet.'[91]

### SAINTE-BAUME IN THE HOGGAR*

Ever since Moses' meeting with God at Horeb in Sinai,

*Sainte-Baume: a mountain, 1147 m, to the north of Toulon in southern France (Provence); the Hoggar or Ahaggar: the south-easterly region of Algeria, bordering on Nigeria, where Charles de Foucauld lived (Tamanrasset) from 1905 to his death in 1916. Trans. note.

57

to adore the Lord and contemplate his face one must go up the mountain alone. The contemplative tradition in the Church, since St John of the Cross, has called this lofty seat of contemplation Mount Carmel, in remembrance of the prophet Elijah.

Brother Charles of Jesus called it Mount Sainte-Baume, because of a Provençale tradition that Mary Magdalene spent the last years of her life on Sainte-Baume, given up entirely to contemplation and the pure love of God. Attributing the gesture of Mary, Lazarus' sister, to Mary Magdalene, Charles de Foucauld imagined her at Bethany bringing in 'a pound of very costly ointment, pure nard' and anointing Jesus' feet with it (Jn 12 :3). 'She gave You the whole of herself, totally . . . everything she was and had, as she was to do later on Sainte-Baume.'[92]

This symbolic mountain, Sainte-Baume, was Brother Charles' image for the Christian's vocation and destiny : 'Eternal life is this : to know you, the only true God, and Jesus Christ whom you have sent' (Jn 17 :3).

How many Christians, alas, carried away by the modern world with its fear of solitude and silence, forget this essential truth of their faith: that the Christian's vocation is 'to know God as He has revealed Himself, to adore Him in contemplation, and to love Him with all one's heart'. They should ponder the following lines, written by Charles de Foucauld from Tamanrasset to Marie de Bondy on 16 January 1912 : 'The soul is made not for noise but for recollection, and life should be a preparation for heaven not only in meritorious works but in peace and recollection in God. Man, however, is immersed in endless discussion; the lack of true joy he finds in noise should more than convince him that he has wandered far from his vocation.'[93]

Like the Israelites, Moses, the prophets and many of

the saints, the Christian 'must go through the desert and sojourn there to receive God's grace: there must be this period of self-emptying in which he purifies himself of all that is not God . . . In this solitude, in this desert life, alone with God . . . God gives Himself to him totally, if he in his turn will give himself totally to God.'[94]

Charles de Foucauld carried out his own advice. Leaving Sainte-Baume on the morning of 9 September 1901, he set sail from Marseilles at midday, and for the next fifteen years, until his death, he lived in the desert, firstly at Beni-Abbès and then in the Hoggar: from Sainte-Baume to Asekrem.*

Charles de Foucauld's journey was real; but it is also a perfect symbol for his lonely, silent pilgrimage towards God, this God whom man in his knowledge and love can never exhaust.

Jesus said to him: 'You must destroy in yourself everything that is not God . . . make yourself a desert here, where you can be alone with Me like Mary Magdalene.'[95]

What desert is this? Where is the hidden path that leads not to the high places of the earth, Horeb, Sainte-Baume or Asekrem, but to the high place where the soul is alone with Jesus, the high place in the soul itself where God dwells?

This desert, this hidden path are pure faith and hope.

The start of the journey is prayer, long and silent, humble and persevering, absorbed in adoration and love. 'Many days and nights in front of the Blessed Sacrament . . . hours of silence at the feet of the Sacred Host . . .' 'Sweet Sainte-Baume' he called it in a letter written on 21 January 1904, when he was crossing the desert in a caravan between Beni-Abbès and Adrar. 'I feel I am doing God's will, and I am at peace; but how I long for

*Asekrem: 2804 m, one of the three highest mountains in the Atakor range, which covers the central Hoggar. Trans. note.

days of solitude at the foot of the Tabernacle! How sweet Sainte-Baume seems!'[96]

Urged on by Jesus' saving love, he penetrates further and further into the desert to be alone, 'in God's care', as he himself writes. And he adds: 'I am the happiest man on earth. What a delicious way to spend one's time, all alone with Jesus.'[97] What pure faith he must have needed to persevere in this daily solitude. As early as 6 June 1897, he wrote in an exercise book of 'spiritual notes': 'I must cling to the life of faith, come what may.'[98] How profoundly true those words must have been, for ten years of 'dryness and darkness' in the Hoggar. Nineteen years later he wrote to Louis Massignon from Tamanrasset: 'Love consists not in feeling that one loves, but in *wanting to love*; when one wishes to love, one loves; when one wishes to love with all one's heart and strength, one loves with all one's heart and strength.'[99] These words reveal the unshakeable faith of his soul.

Day after day he lived entirely alone, in perfect peace, but threatened by the violence of men – from the beginning he had no illusions about the dangers he ran[100] – by disease and famine in an arid land. His only guardians were Jesus and God. His life was one of pure unutterable hope.

Three texts are particularly suitable for revealing the extraordinary peace he experienced. All three occur in letters to Mme de Bondy, but they were written over a period of ten years. In 1906 he wrote:

'Five days ago I was bitten by an adder. As I managed to treat myself straight away, I don't think I'm in any danger . . . Usually when prompt action is taken like that, it soon heals up and one is none the worse . . . But I have to admit that my foot is hurting rather a lot, and I suppose it might turn septic. Jesus will take care of me.'[101]

60

Two years later, after an illness, he wrote :

'Don't worry if I'm ill occasionally and on my own;
God is there. He can help directly as well as through
other people. I was completely at peace.'[102]

And lastly this magnificent text, written the year he died :

'I've only just realised I'm almost deaf in my right
ear . . . My left ear will probably go as well, sooner
or later. Deafness is a handicap hermits long for.'[103]

We glimpse his perfect peace, watched over by the One
he loves and who loves him, his unchangeable peace
which can be found only on the very summit of the
mountain.

'I want to live above the clouds, to leave the earth
behind and live in heaven like St Mary Magdalene on
Sainte-Baume.'[104]
'This Sainte-Baume, which is often the soul's most imperious need, and often the culmination of life on
earth.[105]

## MY FATHER WHO IS ALSO YOUR FATHER

It was on the road of pure faith and hope, in the desert
'in God's care', that Charles experienced for himself
something his faith had revealed to him from the beginning : that God is his Father, the Father of Jesus Christ
and our Father. It was also the fruit of his perfect
imitation of his beloved Brother and Lord Jesus, his total
identification with Jesus, pursued day by day from Nazareth to Tamanrasset. The Lord poured himself out into
Charles' soul, giving him that sense of filial love which

he expressed in the so-called prayer of abandonment. Such prayer can cast more light on God's fatherhood, as a living reality, than hours of meditation.

It is, I suppose, much more than a prayer. It is the expression of his whole state of mind, of the very deepest attitudes of his being, with regard to God his Father.

As an example, here is a short extract from one of his meditations on the Gospel, written probably during his time as a Trappist at Akbes monastery in Syria. It is perhaps helpful to place it side by side with some of Jesus' own words. This will show how close to the Gospel his own prayer was.

| | |
|---|---|
| 'My Father, | Father, said Jesus |
| 'I surrender myself to you; do with me what you will. | Yes, Father, that is what it has pleased you to do. I am not alone, because whatever the Father does the Son does too. |
| 'Whatever you do with me, I am grateful. | If you know how to give your children what is good, how much more will your Father in heaven give good things to those who ask him? |
| 'I am ready for everything, I accept everything. | |
| 'If only your will is done in me 'and in all creatures, I want nothing else, my God. | Your kingdom come, your will be done, on earth as in heaven. Father, let your will be done, not mine. |

| | |
|---|---|
| 'I place my soul in your hands; | Into your hands I commit my spirit. |
| 'I give it to you, my God, with all the love in my heart, because I adore you, | The world must be brought to know that I love the Father and that I am doing exactly what the Father told me. |
| 'and because in my love I need to give myself to you, | My food is to do the will of the one who sent me. |
| 'to resign myself utterly into your hands | Anybody who loves me will be loved by my Father. |
| with infinite confidence | There is no need to be afraid, little flock, for it has pleased your Father to give you the kingdom. |
| 'for you are my Father.' | My Father who is also your Father. |

Having surrendered himself utterly to God, Charles of Jesus is 'in the Father's care', and 'no one can steal from the Father' (Jn 10:29).


## WHY DEATH?

The mystery that most exercises the Christian's faith is the mystery of his own death. It comes to us all. But if he thinks about it, what is he to think? Does he welcome death? What did Brother Charles think?

He had felt deeply what separation from one's loved

ones can mean, and on his own admission the greatest sacrifice of his life was when he left his family, and especially Marie de Bondy who had brought him back to God, on 15 January 1890, as he then thought, for good.

This goes a long way to explaining why he never speaks of death as a separation from those one loves on earth. Having willed 'to be buried in our Saviour', he is already dead to the world, and in 1891 he wrote:

'I should just love to go to Jesus soon, but I don't see any hope of it yet . . . May his will be done entirely, whether I remain here a long time or a short time. But this doesn't stop me thinking – on the contrary – what a great day it will be when he calls us; our love would be pretty poor if we didn't long to see him. On the night before the Pasch he himself longed to see his Father.'[106]

The years passed. On 20 July 1914 he wrote:

'I cannot say I want to die; once I did; but now I see so much good that needs to be done, so many souls without a shepherd, that I want to do a little good and work a little for the salvation of these poor souls: but God loves them more than I do, and he doesn't need me. May his will be done.'[107]

These emotions are not at all contradictory, because they are both inspired by love: love for God and love for man. Many of the saints expressed similar feelings, not least St Paul himself (Ph 1 : 21–6).

What is less usual, and rarely expressed with such strength of feeling, is the desire for martyrdom.

In a meditation from his Nazareth retreat of 1897, he imagined the Lord's saying to him:

'Death will come to you. You say you want martyrdom . . . you know you are weak . . . but you also
know that you can do anything in Him who strength-
ens you, that I am all-powerful in My creatures . . .
Ask for martyrdom day and night, always on the condition that it is My will (...) and have confidence, I
shall do what you ask, I shall do what gives Me the
greatest glory . . . But to ask for that is good, because
it is "the sign of the greatest love to give one's life for
what one loves", and it is perfectly right for you to want
to give Me the "sign of the greatest love".'[108]

And in a meditation on the passion he wrote :

'In Your name, O my Beloved, I beg the grace to shed
my blood for You, lovingly, courageously, giving You
the greatest glory possible.'[109]

From that moment his daily life was not a preparation
for death; it was a preparation for martyrdom.
The resolutions of his Beni-Abbès retreat often end :

'To prepare oneself constantly for martyrdom, and
accept it without a shadow of reluctance like the divine
Lamb, in Jesus, through Jesus, for Jesus.'[110]

For Charles of Jesus, then, martyrdom is at once an
imitation of Jesus in his painful and violent death, a way
of giving the sign of the greatest love, and union with the
One he loves.
His daily life in the fraternity at Beni-Abbès was like
waiting for something that is going to happen very soon :

'I must try and live as if I were to die a martyr today.
Every minute I must imagine I am going to be martyred this very evening.'[111]

Right up to the evening of 1 December 1916 at Taman-rasset, his wish was exactly the same.

A little pocket-book of his, a sort of jotter, starts with the same words : 'My wish is to live as if I were to die a martyr today', and it ends with three prayers repeating the same earnest desire.

'My Lord Jesus, You said, "A man can have no greater love than to lay down his life for his friends". With all my heart I want to lay down my life for You. This is my most fervent prayer.'

In the second prayer, he adds after 'I want to give my life for You' :

'Thank you for the hope of martyrdom You have given me.'[112]

### CONCLUSION

This account of the great insights of Brother Charles' faith has not been exhaustive. It has simply intended to reveal something of the depths of his mind as we can glean them from his writings and life. As we conclude, we cannot help being struck by how totally his life is saturated with the Gospel. All his spiritual ideas are inspired by a Gospel phrase. In silence at the feet of Jesus he listens to the Word, meditating on it all day long and living it out to the letter. It is this which makes Charles de Foucauld a disciple of Jesus.

He followed Jesus 'as closely as possible', 'living always with Him' for thirty years – the same length of time that Jesus spent hidden at Nazareth. At the evening of a life sealed with his blood, Charles de Foucauld had perfectly

66

fulfilled his vocation. As he imagined Jesus himself to have told him in one of his meditations:

'Your vocation is to shout the Gospel from the roof-tops, not in words, but with your life.'[113]

# PART THREE

*Extracts from the Writings of
Brother Charles of Jesus*

MEDITATION ON SELF-ABASEMENT

*Nazareth, November 1897*

'My Lord Jesus, may I dare to ask You to do this meditation for me? You Yourself said: "The disciple is not
superior to his teacher, nor the slave to his master" . . . .
You are telling me not to be above You in the eyes of
men here below . . . How can I practise self-abasement? . . .

'First of all notice that after I said, "The slave is not
superior to his master", I added: "It is enough for the
disciple that he should grow to be like his teacher." I don't
want you to be superior to what I was, but I don't want
you to be inferior either . . . If there are exceptions, they're
not for you, because your vocation, as I've told you often,
is the perfect imitation of Me, Me alone . . . Try then to
be in the eyes of the world what I was when I lived at
Nazareth, neither more nor less. I was a poor workman,
living by the work of My hands; I was considered unlettered and uneducated; My parents, relations and
friends were all workers like Me, artisans, fishermen; I
was their equal; I was dressed like them, lodged like them,
I ate like them when I was with them . . . Like all poor
people, I was the butt of contempt, and it is because in
the eyes of the world I was just 'that poor Nazareen'
that I was so persecuted, so ill-treated in My public life,
that at My first preaching in the synagogue at Nazareth
I was nearly thrown off the cliff; that I was called Beel-
zebul in Galilee, and possessed in Judaea; that I was treat-

ed like an imposter and adventurer, and put to death on a gibbet between two thieves; I was dismissed as a vulgar careerist ... Let people think of you what they thought of Me, my child: unlettered, poor, a commoner; and what you really are, unintelligent, without talent or virtue; always look for the basest occupations; but try to develop your intelligence under the direction of your confessor, but in secret, unknown to the world; I was infinitely wise, but nobody knew it; don't be afraid to learn, it's good for your soul; study diligently, to improve, to know Me better, to love Me more, to know My will and fulfil it better, to imitate Me, perfect Knowledge, better: be very ignorant in men's eyes, very knowledgeable in divine learning, at the foot of my Tabernacle ... I was little and infinitely despised; look for, ask for, cherish the jobs which abase you most, raking manure, digging the ground, anything low and common: the smaller you are, the more you will be like Me ... Let people think you mad, it doesn't matter, thank Me for it: I was thought mad, and it'll help you to imitate Me ... Let them throw stones, laugh at you, shout insults at you in the street, so much the better! Thank Me for it, it is an infinite grace I give you, because didn't I get the same treatment? ... You should think yourself very fortunate if I give you this measure of imitation ... ! But do nothing eccentric or bizarre to deserve insults; I did nothing, I did not deserve the treatment meted out to me, far from it; and yet I was ill-used; don't you do anything to deserve ill-treatment, but if I give you the grace to suffer it, thank Me for it; don't try to prevent it or stop it; bear it all with joy, and be very grateful to Me for giving it you like a brother's gift ... Do everything I would have done, do everything I did; do nothing but good, and devote yourself to the most disagreeable and humbling jobs; in everything you do – the way you dress, how you live,

72

the considerate and brotherly way you treat the little ones of the earth – show people you are the equal of the smallest . . . Do your best to hide anything which might raise you in your neighbour's estimation.'

*Ecrits spirituels*, pp. 108–11

### JESUS IN THE HOLY EUCHARIST

*Nazareth, November 1897*

'My Lord Jesus, You are present in the Holy Eucharist. You are there, three feet from me, in the Tabernacle. Your Body, Your soul, Your humanity, Your entire being is there in its two natures; how close You are, my Saviour, my Jesus, my Brother, my Spouse, my Beloved! . . . You were no closer to our Lady during the nine months she carried You than You are to me when You come on my tongue in Communion. You were no closer to our Lady and St Joseph in the stable at Bethlehem, in the house at Nazareth, on the flight into Egypt, at any moment of that divine family life, than You are to me at this instant and so, so often in this tabernacle! (...) How happy I am! . . . It is the greatest sweetness to be alone in my cell and converse with You in the silence of the night; You are there as God and by Your grace; but to stay in my cell when I could be before the Blessed Sacrament is as if St Mary Magdalene, when you were at Bethany, went off and left You alone . . . to think about You, alone in her room . . . To kiss the places You sanctified in Your mortal life: the stones of Gethsemane and Calvary, the soil of the Via Dolorosa, the waters of the Sea of Galilee, is a sweet and pious thing to do, my God, but to prefer that to your Tabernacle is to leave Jesus living at my side, to leave Him alone, and go off somewhere on my own to venerate dead stones where He is not; it is to leave the room He is in and His divine companionship to go and kiss the floor of a room He was in but is no longer . . . Leaving the Tabernacle to go and venerate statues is leaving Jesus living near me and going into another room to pay my respects to His picture (...)

'Wherever the Sacred Host is, there the living God is, your Saviour, as really as when He was living and speaking in Galilee and Judaea and as He is now in Heaven . . . Never miss communion through your own fault: one communion is more than life, more than all the wealth of the world, more than the entire universe, it is God Himself, it is Me, Jesus. Can you prefer anything to Me? If you love Me however little, can you voluntarily lose the grace I give you when I come to you in communion? . . . Love Me with the fulness and wholeness of your heart.'

*Ecrits spirituels,* pp. 69–71

*Beni-Abbès, 12 September 1902*   To Marie de Bondy

'The marvellous thing about Beni-Abbès is the sunsets, the evenings and the nights. When I see the magnificent sunsets, I always remember how fond you are of them because they remind you of the great peace that will follow the storm of our life on earth. The evenings are so calm, the nights so serene, the great arc of the sky and those vast horizons glistening with the flickering stars so peaceful and singing such silent, radiant praises of the Eternal, the Infinite, the beyond, that I could spend whole nights just gazing in contemplation; I cut my gazing short, however, and soon return to the tabernacle, because there is more in the humble tabernacle. Everything is worthless compared with the Beloved.'

*Lettres à Mme de Bondy,* pp. 105–6

*Jerusalem, 19 November 1898*   To his sister

'You know, when you are in love, you live less in yourself than in the one you love, and the more you are in
love, the more you live outside yourself, in the one you
love ...

'If we love Jesus, we live much more in Him than in
ourselves, we forget our own affairs and think only of
His, and as He enjoys an unspeakable peace and happiness, seated at His Father's right hand, we share in the
peace and happiness of our Divine Beloved depending
on how much we are in love.'

*Ecrits spirituels,* p. 184

*Beni-Abbès, 23 December 1903*   To Henry de Castries

'Peace and war pass away! God is greater than either,
He alone does not pass away. In the Sacred Heart fraternity, we are not indifferent to things going on outside,
because they bring good or evil to these friends of God;
but when we've done what we can, how peaceful it is to
kneel alone in front of the tabernacle, face to face with
JESUS. What peace there is, what happiness!

'The hermit is always happy, as you can see, dear
friend, and his life is spent in the thought and joy of the
infinite happiness and unchangeable peace of the Blessed
and ever-peaceful Trinity.'

*Lettres à Henry de Castries,* p. 144

*Tamanrasset, 18 November 1907*   To Marie de Bondy

'It is hard not to grieve for all the evil in the world, the small amount of good, the number of enterprising enemies of God, the hesitancy of his friends, and one's own misery (...) And yet we must not grieve, but look above what is going on, towards our Beloved (...) Since his happiness and peace are infinite, perfect, unchangeable, they should flood us with a joy, a peace, a fulness which put to rest all the sadness of our souls at the miseries of the world.'

*Lettres à Mme de Bondy,* pp. 163–4

### TO FOLLOW IN POVERTY A GOD OF POVERTY

*Nazareth, November 1897*

'My Lord Jesus, Your faithful disciple, loving You with all his heart, and loath to see himself richer than his Master, will lose no time in becoming quite poor! . . .

'My Lord Jesus, Your faithful disciple, remembering that anything done for one of these little ones is done for You, and anything not done for them is not done for You, will lose no time in becoming quite poor to alleviate all the wretchedness within his power! . . .

'The man who receives *Your words with faith* : "If you wish to be perfect, go and sell what you own and give the money to the poor . . . How happy are you who are poor, for everyone who has left his goods for the sake of my name will be repaid a hundred times over, and also inherit eternal life . . ." and so many others! will lose no time in becoming quite poor.

'My God, I don't know whether certain souls can see You poor and stay rich themselves, whether they have such a high opinion of themselves over their Master,

76

their Beloved, that they have no wish to imitate You in everything, as far as they can, and especially in Your humiliations; they probably love You very much, my God, but in my view their love is incomplete; I at any rate cannot imagine a love which does not feel the *need*, an *imperious need* to conform with, to resemble and above all to share all the troubles, difficulties and labours of life . . .

'My God, I can't be rich, live in comfort, enjoy my wealth, while You were poor, harassed, living painfully by manual work, I just couldn't . . . I can't love like that . . .

' "The disciple is not superior to his teacher", or the wife richer than her Spouse when He is poor, particularly voluntarily poor, and perfect . . . St Theresa, tired of refusing to accept money for her monastery at Avila, was sometimes on the point of giving in, but when she returned to her oratory and saw the Cross, she fell at his feet and begged Jesus stripped on the cross to give her the grace to refuse all revenues and to be as poor as He . . .

'I judge no one, my God, others are Your servants and my brothers, and I must love them, do good to them and pray for them; but I cannot understand a love that does not struggle to be like You and has no need to share all crosses . . .'

*Ecrits spirituels*, pp. 105–7

LIKE JESUS AT NAZARETH

*17 May 1906, Feast of St Pascal Baylon*   Diary

'For six rest-days from Maundy Thursday to Easter Tuesday, quasi-retreat. Here is a brief synopsis and my resolutions.

'Reminder of the kind of life I am meant to be leading. Imitation of Jesus at Nazareth. Adoration of the exposed Blessed Sacrament : silent sanctification of pagan peoples by bringing Jesus among them.

'His adoration and the imitation of his hidden life.

'Reminder of continual imitation of Jesus in his life at Nazareth.

'Reminder of penance, the narrow way, the cross of Jesus at Nazareth.

'Reminder of Jesus' retreat and silence at Nazareth.

'Reminder of Jesus' self-abasement, humble manual work at Nazareth.

'Reminder of Jesus' retreat and silence at Nazareth.

'Reminder of Jesus' seclusion from the world, and the things of the world, at Nazareth.

'Reminder of Jesus' life of spiritual communion, adoration, prayer and vigils at Nazareth.

'Reminder of zeal for souls in trying to collect round the sacred Host, in these pagan countries, a little family in imitation of Jesus' life at Nazareth.

'Reminder of zeal for souls, in charity, goodness, goodwill to all men, like Jesus at Nazareth.

'Reminder of zeal for souls, in gentleness, humility, forgiveness, quiet acceptance of ill-treatment, like Jesus at Nazareth.

'Reminder of zeal for souls, with one's good example, like Jesus at Nazareth.

'Reminder of zeal for souls in prayer, penance, personal sanctification, like Jesus at Nazareth.

'Reminder to let Jesus' heart live in me, so that it is no longer I who live, but Jesus' heart living in me as he lived at Nazareth.'

*Oeuvres spirituelles*, pp. 375–6

Extract from the Rule of the Little Brothers of the Sacred
Heart, written at Nazareth in 1899 and revised at Beni-
Abbès in 1902.

## Hospitality

'Although we should offer our most careful hospitality
to rich guests and visitors, to retreatants whose piety
makes them especially dear to us as brothers, we are under
an even more pressing obligation to the poor, as we remember these words of Jesus': "When you give a lunch or
dinner, do not ask your friends, brothers, relations or rich
neighbours . . . invite the poor, the crippled, the lame, the
blind." We shall hold the rich in fraternal affection, but
then so many other people hurry to make life pleasant for
them. They are the healthy members of our Lord, where
the poor are his sick and bleeding members; while showing equal respect and equal love to them all, we shall
bandage the wounded limbs before scenting the healthy
ones. The wealthy were rare visitors to the blessed house
at Nazareth; it was the poor who came willingly and con-
fidently; we must see to it that the poor can come con-
fidently to the Fraternity; we shall, of course, welcome
the rich with open arms, but there is no need to expect
them or search them out; we must expect the poor,
though, and make sure everything is ready to offer them
the very best of our hospitality, with enough rooms and
food to cater warmly for numerous guests; our wish must
be to see our houses full; if our guest-rooms are inadequ-

ate, we must make them bigger; they must always reflect the holy poverty and abasement of the house at Nazareth, but they must also reflect its charity.'

*Oeuvres spirituelles,* pp. 459–60

## ON SLAVERY

*Beni-Abbès, 4 February 1902*   To Mgr Guérin

'This is what I say to the slaves: far from preaching flight or revolt, I preach patience and acceptance of their present lot, adding that in time God will give them comfort and freedom, that he will comfort them the faster the better they have served him, that they should set their hearts on the kingdom of God and his righteousness, and all other things will be given them as well; at the same time I do not conceal from my French friends that this slavery is an injustice, a monstrous immorality, and that it is their duty to do all in their power to abolish it (...)

'We are not, it is true, responsible for the government of the country, but we *are* responsible for helping our neighbour as ourselves, to do as we would be done by, and consequently to take all necessary steps to alleviate the sufferings of these unfortunate people: insofar as we do it to one of the least of these brothers of Jesus, we do it to him; insofar as we neglect to do it to one of the least of them, we neglect to do it to him . . . Besides, we are not entitled to be dumb dogs and silent watchmen: we must shout out when we see evil.'

*Oeuvres spirituelles,* pp. 619–21

*Ephraim, 4th Sunday of Lent 1898*

'[Our Lord] : I am the Good Shepherd, I am tireless in my search for the lost sheep, I have told you so a hundred times : *Love Me*! because I have shown such love for you, all of you, my sheep, and *love one another* because your Shepherd loves you all so tenderly ! . . . Be grateful to Me for how I look for you, for My goodness in forgiving you, for my joy when I find you. *Help Me in my work, do as I do,* do all you can, with Me and like Me, each according to the advice of his spiritual director, to bring as many lost sheep back as possible . . . share My thoughts, My sorrow at seeing My sheep wander off, My joy at finding them . . . share My perseverance, My hope, My indulgence in looking for them, My hope which never rejects the possibility of their return; My indulgence in forgiving them . . . share My tenderness for them when they come back . . . far from reproaching and punishing them, I clasp them in My arms and kiss them tenderly, as the father did to his prodigal son.

'So *always hope* that all souls living in this world will come back to the path of goodness, work for this within the limits of obedience, and *be tender* to sinners who return, as you have seen Me to be to so many souls . . . In short, *do for sinners what you would want Me to do for you.*'

*Ecrits spirituels*, pp. 167–8

*Beni-Abbès, 21 November 1903: resolutions made into vows, Christmas 1903*

'I propose to :

  'strive to unite myself to the material creation by offering all living creatures to God and singing a hymn of adoration and thanksgiving, praise and love to Him on their behalf.

  'strive to remain united and devoted, in my whole spiritual life and apostolate, to the Catholic Church, that is : to the holy Pontiff, the bishops, priests, religious congregations and all the faithful who compose it.

  'strive to be united, in my whole spiritual life and apostolate, to all the saints in heaven, in purgatory and on earth.

  'strive to be united, in my whole spiritual life and apostolate, to the nine choirs of Angels, to all they do in heaven in their relations with the Father, Son and Holy Spirit, our Lady their Queen, and all they do on earth in their relations with men.'

*Oeuvres spirituelles,* pp. 572–3

THE CHURCH ON THE EVENING OF SS PETER AND PAUL'S
MARTYRDOM

*Tamanrasset, 30 June 1909*   To Mgr Caron

'Do not be surprised at present storms. The bark of Peter has weathered many others. Think of the evening of the day when SS Peter and Paul were martyred. How sombre everything must have seemed to the little Church of Rome. The first Christians did not lose heart. To us who have eighteen centuries of the Church's life to strengthen our faith, how puny those efforts of hell, of which Jesus said, "they can never hold out", must seem (...) Jesus said to us as well as to his Apostles: "Proclaim the Good News to all creation". There is nothing we cannot master with the help of the One who gives us strength. He has conquered the world; like him we shall *always* have the cross, like him we shall *always* be persecuted, like him we shall *always* be defeated in the eyes of the world, like him we shall *always* triumph in fact, and this to the extent of our faithfulness to grace (...) We are with the *Almighty*, and the only power enemies have is the power it pleases him to give them, to test us, to sanctify us, to give spiritual victory – which is the only true victory, an eternal one – to his Church and his elect.

'Let us return to the Gospel, if we do not live the Gospel, *Jesus does not live in us*.'

*XXV Lettres inédites*, pp. 77–8

### MEDITATION ON THE VISITATION

*Ephraim, Lent 1898*

'When I had scarcely become incarnate, I asked my Mother to take me to the house where John was to be born, so that I could sanctify him before his birth . . . I have given myself to the world for its salvation, in the Incarnation . . . Even before I was born, I was at work for the sanctification of men . . . and I urged my Mother to join with Me . . . She is not the only person I urge to work, to sanctify others, as soon as she possesses me: I ask all souls to do the same when I come to them. One day I shall tell my apostles: "Preach", and I shall give them a mission and outline their rules . . . Here I tell all other souls, all who possess me and live hidden lives but who have not received a mission to preach, I tell them to sanctify souls by taking me among them in silence; to souls of silence, to souls of hidden life, living far from the world in solitude, I say: "All of you, work for the sanctification of the world, as my Mother did, without speaking, in silence; go and set up your pious retreats in the midst of those who do not know me; take me among them by founding an Altar, a Tabernacle, and bring the Gospel to them, preaching it not by word of mouth but by example, not proclaiming it but living it; sanctify the world, take me to the world, pious souls, hidden and silent souls, as Mary took me to John . . .'

*Ecrits spirituels,* pp. 128–9

MARY MAGDALENE

*Beni-Abbès, 1905, Saturday of Passion Week*

'My God, it is on this evening of the last week of your life, an evening of love and pain, an evening of sweetness because You are present, and of pain because You are so near death and such great suffering, it is on this evening that Mary Magdalene anoints your feet and head "to prepare You for burial", as You say Yourself. By pouring out the ointment, by breaking the jar, she pours out over your feet, she gives You totally, her whole being, body and soul, heart and mind: all she is she gives You: she pours out the perfume and breaks the jar . . . she keeps nothing, she gives her all, everything she is and everything she has: as she will do later on Sainte-Baume: without keeping anything of herself, without keeping anything for herself.'

Oeuvres spirituelles, pp. 236–7

### ALONE WITH JESUS

*Tamanrasset, 3 September 1905*  To Marie de Bondy

'Tomorrow morning the French detachment leaves. I shall be well set up: the sale of my camels will enable me to have a simple house built in stone and earth; and a reed hut; to dig a small well and clear a small garden . . . Do not worry: we, you and I, are in the hands of the Beloved . . . He is worth more to us than all the soldiers in the world . . . and your child will share the destiny of our great-great-uncle,* won't you be glad? Jesus said it was the greatest sign of a man's love, wouldn't you be glad to see your child give it? . . . But I don't think it will happen: non sum dignus. The country is thought to be very quiet: I am delighted, and think it's probably true, but there might still be the occasional trouble here and there . . . I shall be alone, happy, very happy, to be alone with Jesus, alone for Jesus.'

Lettres à Mme de Bondy, p. 144

*Nazareth, 14 November 1897, election*

To acquire by divine grace complete detachment from what is not God, poverty of spirit which leaves no little thoughts, no little cares, no little anxieties, no thoughts of personal interest, either material or spiritual, no little con-

*Vicar general of Arles, massacred with the Carmelite monks during the Revolution.

siderations, nothing earthly, petty or vain : to empty the soul totally, and leave nothing but the thought and love of God ... *To live on high, to be no longer of the earth,* to live in heaven like St Mary Magdalene on Sainte-Baume.'

*Ecrits spirituels,* p. 176

## TO MAKE UP ALL THAT HAS STILL TO BE UNDERGONE BY CHRIST

Extract from the Rule of the Little Brothers of the Sacred Heart

'The Little Brothers are to remember each day that one of the favours their Spouse Jesus has lavished on them is the possibility, the firm hope, of ending their life by martyrdom : let them prepare themselves for this happy end : let them behave at each moment as befits souls called by the Spouse's goodness to receive – perhaps soon – this infinite favour ... Their desires and prayers should plead for the blessed moment when they can give their Beloved this greatest sign of their love; they must be always worthy of such a great vocation . . . And when the moment comes, let them, without a shadow of defence (we are forbidden to possess, carry and use weapons), "like sheep among wolves", as meek as the divine Lamb, humble, overflowing with gratitude, praying for their persecutors, letting Jesus make up in their deaths all that he has still to undergo, offering themselves to Him for his greater glory, for all the intentions for which He offered Himself on Calvary, uniting the sacrifice of their lives with the sacrifice of his life, in peace, blessing and love, letting Him live and act in them more than ever at this supreme, blessed hour, called as they are to imitate Him in his death

86

as in his life, shed their blood and exhale their souls in Jesus, by Jesus, like Jesus, for Jesus!'

*Oeuvres spirituelles,* p. 788


### YOUR THOUGHT OF DEATH

'Think that you are going to die a martyr, stripped of everything, stretched out on the ground, naked, hardly recognisable, covered with blood and wounds, violently and painfully killed . . . and wish it to be today. If I am to grant you this infinite grace, be vigilant and carry the cross faithfully. Consider that your whole life must come to such an end : and understand the scant importance of many things. Think of this death often, prepare yourself for it and judge things at their true value.'

*Ecrits spirituels,* pp. 172–3

# PART FOUR

with indications of his main writings.

1858 On 15 September, Charles Eugène Viscount de
Foucauld is born at Strasbourg.
Both his parents die before he is seven.
At the age of sixteen, he loses his faith.

1876 Enters the Special Military School, which at that
time was still at Saint-Cyr near Versailles.

After a brilliant academic career, Lieutenant de
Foucauld leaves for Algeria in 1880. He is dismissed
from the army in 1881 for 'indiscipline and notorious
misconduct', but requests readmission on learning that
his regiment is fighting insurgents at Bou-Amama in
the southern Oranais. The campaign over, he resigns
his commission.

1883–4 For two years he undertakes a fruitful but dangerous
mission, the results of which are published as *Recon-
naissance au Maroc*.

1886 February, settles in Paris.
After a period of search and questioning, he is suddenly
converted in October of that year, at the age of
twenty-eight. At the house of his aunt, Madame
Moitessier, Charles de Foucauld meets Fr Huvelin
who was especially instrumental in his return to the
faith. Until Fr Huvelin's death he carried on a close
*Correspondence* with this 'spiritual father' and 'best
friend'. At his aunt's he also meets his cousin Marie,
Madame de Bondy, to whom he is later able to write :

'God made you the first instrument of his mercies to me.' His *Correspondence* with Mme de Bondy – to whom he had promised to reveal his inmost thoughts – ends only with his death.

1890 16 January, Viscount de Foucauld enters the Cistercians at Our Lady of the Snows in the Ardèche (southeast France), where for six months he is a novice under the name of Brother Marie-Albéric. Having asked to be sent to the poorest Cistercian monastery, he is sent on 17 June 1890 to Our Lady of the Sacred Heart at Akbes in Syria, where he remains until February 1897.

Irresistibly attracted to a more perfect imitation of 'that little life of Nazareth' which he is 'pained to see Jesus leading alone', he leaves the Cistercians on 14 February 1897 after the Abbot General of the Order has ratified his hermit's vocation. Fr. de Foucauld was to retain good friends among the Cistercians, as his *Letters to my Cistercian Brothers* witness.

1897 4 March, Brother Charles of Jesus arrives at Nazareth, where he becomes servant-cum-gardener-cum-odd-job-man for the Poor Clares : 'This is the very life I have been looking for.' He was to remain for nearly three years.

His *Meditations*, notably on the Gospel, and his retreat *Notes* (the most important being written at Nazareth in November 1897) date from this period in the Holy Land. Although not destined for publication, they form the bulk of the *Spiritual Writings* of Fr de Foucauld.

1898 *Notes* from a week's 'Lenten retreat at Ephraim' in southern Palestine.

1900 22 September, Charles de Foucauld returns to France, and on the 29th he re-enters Our Lady of the Snows to begin his ordination retreat. He is ordained priest by Mgr Bonnet, bishop of Viviers, on 9 June 1901.

In September he leaves for Africa.

1901 28 October, arrives at Beni-Abbès, where he is the only priest for 250 miles. In his hermitage he sleeps on the bare ground, and lives on bread and boiled barley. He spends all his days at prayer.

In the Sahara his meditation notes become fewer and his retreat notes simpler. On the other hand the volume of his correspondence increases : *letters* to his bishop Mgr Guérin; to old friends such as Henry de Castries; to new acquaintances like Monsieur Massignon and Mgr Caron, superior of the minor seminary of Versailles; to soldiers on active service in the Oases; and so forth.

At Beni-Abbès Brother Charles writes twenty-one catechetical talks which make up the *Gospel presented to the poor of the Sahara* (1903), and finishes (1902) his *Rule of the Little Brothers of the Sacred Heart of Jesus* which he began in 1899 at Nazareth.

At Tamanrasset he writes (1909–13) the 'Statutes for the Association of Brothers and Sisters of the Sacred Heart of Jesus', addressed to evangelising lay-people and better known as the *Directory*.

1905 Moves to Tamanrasset.

1916 1 December, Brother Charles of Jesus is 'violently and painfully killed' by Sanusiyya (Senousis) terrorists afraid of his influence as a priest and a Frenchman. Foreseeing his own 'painful death' in 1897, he added : 'Think of this death often, to prepare yourself for it and judge things at their true value.'

## BIBLIOGRAPHY

### 1. Collections of works by Fr. de Foucauld

*Ecrits spirituels de Charles de Foucauld*. Paris: Gigord, 1923, 1947.
*Nouveaux Ecrits spirituels*. Paris: Plon, 1950.
*Oeuvres spirituelles* (Anthologie). Paris: Seuil, 1958.
*Lettres et Carnets*. Paris: Seuil, 1966.
*Père de Foucauld–Abbé Huvelin*, correspondence inedite. Tournai: Desclée, 1957.
*Lettres à Madame de Bondy*. Paris: Desclée de Brouwer, 1966.
*Lettres à Henry de Castries*. Paris: Grasset, 1938.
*Lettres à mes frères de la Trappe*. Paris: Cerf, 1969.
*Pensées et Maximes*. Paris: La Colombe, 1953.
*Directoire* (1909–13 text). Paris: Seuil, 1961.

### 2. Biographies and Studies

Anne Freemantle. *Desert Calling: The Story of Charles de Foucauld.* London and New York, 1950.
Elizabeth Hamilton. *The Desert My Dwelling Place*. London, 1965.
Margaret Trouncer. *Charles de Foucauld*. London, 1972.

The spiritual tradition of Charles de Foucauld is exemplified and lived out today by the Little Brothers of Jesus, The Little Brothers of the Gospel, and The Little Sisters of Jesus. These communities were founded by René Voillaume, who has contributed the preface to this book. The following books by Fr. Voillaume are available in English.

*Seeds of the Desert*. London, 1964.
*Brothers of Men*. London and Denville, New Jersey, 1966.
*The Need for Contemplation*. London and Denville, New Jersey, 1972.
*Christian Vocation*. London and Denville, New Jersey, 1973.
*Faith and Contemplation*. London and Denville, New Jersey, 1974.

Other books by Little Brothers embodying the spirituality of Charles de Foucauld available in English:

Carlo Carretto. *Letters from the Desert*. London and Maryknoll, New York, 1972.
Carlo Carretto. *The God Who Comes*. London and Maryknoll, New York, 1974.
Arturo Paoli. *The Freedom to Be Free*. Maryknoll, New York, 1973.

1. Letter, 29 July 1895, quoted by R. Bazin in his *Charles de Foucauld*.
2. *Lettres à Henry de Castries*, p. 100.
3. Ibid., p. 94.
4. Letter, 8 July 1901, ibid., p. 86.
5. Letter, 14 August 1901, ibid., p. 96.
6. These two documents are admirably analysed by Jean-François Six in his *Itinéraire*, chap. 2.
7. Bossuet's *Elévations sur les Mystères*, which his cousin Marie de Bondy had given him for his first communion in 1872. He was to say later: 'It was the first Christian book I read before my conversion, and it showed me that the Christian religion could perhaps be true.'
8. His cousin Marie de Bondy.
9. The full text will be found in *Ecrits spirituels*, pp. 74–85. (At Nazareth Charles de Foucauld lived in a wooden lean-to hut against the convent wall, where the Poor Clares had kept the garden tools. During his retreat, which lasted from 5 to 15 November 1897, he meditated either in his cell or in the convent chapel. This explains the many allusions to the Blessed Sacrament in this retreat. See *Ecrits spirituels*, p. 45. Trans. note.)
10. Letter, 14 August 1901, *Lettres à Henry de Castries*, pp. 95–6.
11. Ibid., p. 100.

12. Meditations on the Gospel, *Oeuvres spirituelles*, p. 147.
13. Retreat at Nazareth, November 1897, *Ecrits spirituels*, p. 88.
14. Retreat at Nazareth, *Oeuvres spirituelles*, pp. 523–4.
15. Quoted by J.-F. Six, *Itinéraire*, p. 93.
16. Meditations on the Gospel, *Oeuvres spirituelles*, p. 173.
17. Letter, 14 August 1901, *Lettres à Henry de Castries*, p. 97.
18. Meditations on the Gospel, *Oeuvres spirituelles*, p. 166.
19. Ibid., pp. 147–8.
20. Meditations on the Gospel, *Ecrits spirituels*, pp. 38–9.
21. Letter to Louis de Foucauld, 12 April 1897, *Oeuvres spirituelles*, p. 32.
22. Letter to Mme de Bondy, 19 March 1896, *Lettres à Mme de Bondy*, p. 58.
23. Ibid., p. 60.
24. Letter to Louis de Foucauld, loc. cit., p. 32.
25. Retreat at Nazareth, *Ecrits spirituels*, p. 24.
26. Cf. Meditation on the Gospel, *Oeuvres spirituelles*, p. 268.
27. Letter to Mgr Caron, 8 April 1905, *XXV Lettres inédites du P. de Foucauld*, Bonne Presse, Paris, n.d., pp. 14–15.
28. Letter to Fr Jérôme, 28 January 1898, *Lettres à mes frères de la Trappe*, p. 130.
29. Meditations on the Gospel, *Oeuvres spirituelles*, p. 790.
30. *L'Evangile présenté aux Pauvres du Sahara*, Arthaud, Paris 1937, 21st talk, p. 145.
31. Retreat at Beni-Abbès 1902, *Ecrits spirituels*, p. 210.
32. *L'Evangile présenté aux Pauvres du Sahara* (see note 30 above), ibid.
33. Letter to Fr Huvelin, 26 April 1901, *Père de Foucauld-Abbé Huvelin*, pp. 135–6.
34. Diaconate retreat, 23 March 1901, quoted by J.-F. Six, *Itinéraire*, p. 362.

35. Letter, Easter Tuesday 1891, *Lettres à Mme de Bondy*, p. 35.
36. *Ecrits spirituels*, pp. 67–8.
37. Detached notes, *Oeuvres spirituelles*, p. 324.
38. Letter, 5 November 1902, *Lettres à Mme de Bondy*, p. 107.
39. Letter to his sister, *Ecrits spirituels*, p. 228.
40. *Lettres à Henry de Castries*, p. 157.
41. Retreat at Nazareth, *Ecrits spirituels*, p. 86.
42. Quoted in J.-F. Six, *Itinéraire*, p. 360.
43. Letter to Louis Massignon, *Oeuvres spirituelles*, p. 143.
44. Meditations on the Gospel, ibid., p. 93.
45. Meditation on Lk 6:40: 'The disciple is not superior to his teacher', *Oeuvres spirituelles*, p. 206.
46. Cf. *Oeuvres spirituelles*, pp. 602–3.
47. Retreat at Nazareth, *Ecrits spirituels*, p. 106.
48. Ibid., p. 105.
49. Retreat at Nazareth, ibid., p. 105.
50. Meditation on the Gospel, *Oeuvres spirituelles*, p. 215.
51. Ibid., p. 778.
52. Rule of the Little Brothers of the Sacred Heart, ibid., p. 460.
53. Ibid., p. 458.
54. Letter to Marie de Bondy, 7 January 1902, quoted by J.-F. Six, *Itinéraire*, p. 275.
55. Letter to Mgr Guérin, 19 January 1902, ibid.
56. Letter to Mgr Guérin, 28 June 1902, *Oeuvres spirituelles*, p. 621.
57. Letter to Dom Martin, 7 February 1902, *Lettres à mes frères de la Trappe*, p. 224.
58. Meditations on the Passion, *Oeuvres spirituelles*, pp. 266 and 262–3.
59. Meditations on the Gospel, ibid., p. 197.
60. Cf. Retreat at Nazareth, *Ecrits spirituels*, pp. 55–65.
61. *XXV Lettres inédites* (see note 27 above), p. 13.

62. *Ecrits spirituels*, p. 66.

63. Cf. Diary, *Oeuvres spirituelles*, p. 346.

64. Letter to Mgr Guérin, 30 September 1902, Ibid., p. 683.

65. Ibid., p. 490.

66. Letter to a Friend, 15 January 1906, *Ecrits spirituels*, p. 234.

67. Letter to Marie de Bondy, 5 November 1902, quoted by René Bazin in his *Charles de Foucauld*, p. 231.

68. *Ecrits spirituels*, p. 244.

69. Retreat at Nazareth, *Oeuvres spirituelles*, pp. 523-4.

70. Diary for 1903, ibid., p. 346.

71. Retreat at Beni-Abbès 1902, ibid., p. 547.

72. Ibid., p. 549.

73. *Ecrits spirituels*, p. 233.

74. Letter to Fr Jérôme, *Lettres à mes frères de la Trappe*, p. 139.

75. *Père de Foucauld-Abbé Huvelin*, p. 219.

76. Ibid.

77. Retreat at Ephraim, Lent 1898, *Ecrits spirituels*, p. 136.

78. Cf. *Oeuvres spirituelles*, pp. 289-90.

79. Letter, 12 January 1909, *Lettres à Mme Bondy*, p. 177.

80. Letter to Mgr Guérin, 27 February 1903, *Ecrits spirituels*, p. 230. On p. 82-3 of the present work the reader will find a related text on the Church.

81. Letter to Mgr Guérin, 30 September 1902, *Oeuvres spirituelles*, p. 682.

82. Meditation on the Gospel, ibid., p. 93.

83. Ibid., p. 13.

84. Retreat at Nazareth, *Ecrits spirituels*, p. 85.

85. Retreat 1902, ibid., p. 210.

86. *Lettres à Mme de Bondy*, p. 146.

87. See Meditation on the Visitation on p. 83-4 of the present work.

88. *Lettres à Mme de Bondy*. p. 76.

89. *XXV Lettres inédites* (see note 27 above), p. 46.

90. See Meditation on St Mary Magdalene on p. 84–5 of the present work.

91. *Ecrits spirituels*, p. 5.

92. Meditations on the Gospel, *Oeuvres spirituelles*, p. 237.

93. *Lettres à Mme de Bondy*, p. 205.

94. Letter to Fr Jérôme, 19 May 1898, *Lettres à mes frères de la Trappe*, pp. 142–3.

95. Retreat at Nazareth, *Ecrits spirituels*, p. 119.

96. *Lettres à Mme de Bondy*, p. 124.

97. Letter to Mgr Guérin, 2 April 1906, *Ecrits spirituels*, p. 234.

98. Ibid., pp. 170–1.

99. Letter to Louis Massignon, 15 July 1916, *Oeuvres spirituelles*, p. 177.

100. Letter to Mme de Bondy, 3 September 1905, on p. 85 of the present work.

101. Letter to Mme de Bondy, 16 August, *Lettres à Mme de Bondy*, p. 151.

102. Letter to Marie Bondy, 16 May 1908, ibid., p. 169.

103. Letter to Marie de Bondy, 29 January 1916, ibid., p. 241.

104. *Ecrits spirituels*, p. 176.

105. Letter to Louis Massignon, 5 April 1909, *Oeuvres spirituelles*, p. 767. It is in this letter, written at Beni-Abbès that Fr de Foucauld refers to 'Sainte-Baume in the Hoggar'.

106. Letter, 16 July 1891, *Lettres à Mme de Bondy*, p. 36.

107. Letter, 20 July 1914, ibid., p. 229.

108. Retreat at Nazareth, *Ecrits spirituels*, p. 86.

109. *Oeuvres spirituelles*, p. 285.

110. *Ecrits spirituels*, p. 213.

111. Ibid.

112. *Oeuvres spirituelles*, p. 48.

113. Retreat at Nazareth, November 1897, *Ecrits spirituels*, p. 121.